Best TALL Buildings 2010:
CTBUH International Award Winning Projects

Edited by Antony Wood

Council on Tall Buildings and Urban Habitat, Chicago

Council on Tall Buildings and Urban Habitat

Routledge
Taylor & Francis Group
NEW YORK AND LONDON

Routledge
Taylor & Francis Group

NEW YORK AND LONDON

Editor: Antony Wood
Coordinating Editor & Design: Steven Henry

First published 2011 by Routledge
2 Park Square, Milton Park, Abingdon, Oxon, OX14 4RN

Simultaneously published in the USA and Canada by Routledge
270 Madison Avenue, New York, NY 10016

Routledge is an imprint of the Taylor & Francis Group, an informa business

Published in conjunction with the Council of Tall Buildings and Urban Habitat (CTBUH) and the Illinois Institute of Technology

British Library Cataloguing in Publication Data
A catalogue record for this book is available from the British Library

Library of Congress Cataloging-in-Publication Data
A catalog record for this book has been applied for

ISBN13 978-0-415-59404-2
ISSN 1948-1012

Council on Tall Buildings and Urban Habitat
S.R. Crown Hall
Illinois Institute of Technology
3360 South State Street
Chicago, IL 60616
Phone: +1 (312) 567-3487
Fax: +1 (312) 567-3820
Email: info@ctbuh.org
http://www.ctbuh.org

Acknowledgments:

The CTBUH would like to thank all the companies who submitted their projects for consideration for the 2010 awards program and who contributed to the content of this book.

We would also like to thank our 2010 Awards Committee members for volunteering their time and efforts in deliberating this year's winners.

Contents

Foreword, *Gordon Gill* — 6
Introduction — 8
Best Tall Building Awards Criteria — 18

Best Tall Building Americas:

Winner:
The Bank of America Tower, *New York* — 22

Finalists:
Aqua Tower, *Chicago* — 28
One Madison Park, *New York* — 32
Veer Towers, *Las Vegas* — 36

Nominees:
100 11th Avenue, *New York* — 40
235 Van Buren, *Chicago* — 42
300 East Randolph, *Chicago* — 44
785 Eighth Avenue, *New York* — 46
1450 Brickell, *Miami* — 47
Banco Real Santander Headquarters, *São Paulo* — 48
Cassa, *New York* — 49
The Clare at Water Tower, *Chicago* — 50
Fairmont Pacific Rim, *Vancouver* — 51
Freeport-McMoRan Center, *Phoenix* — 52
LA Live Hotel and Residences, *Los Angeles* — 54
The Legacy, *Chicago* — 56
Mandarin Oriental, *Las Vegas* — 57
RBC Centre, *Toronto* — 58
Sackville-Dundas Residences, *Toronto* — 59
Shangri-la, *Vancouver* — 60
The Standard, *New York* — 62
theWit Hotel, *Chicago* — 63
Titanium La Portada, *Santiago* — 64
Toren, *New York* — 66
Torre Libertad, *Mexico City* — 67
Vdara Hotel & Spa, *Las Vegas* — 68
Ventura Corporate Towers, *Rio de Janeiro* — 69
William Beaver House, *New York* — 70

1075 Peachtree, *Atlanta* — 72
353 North Clark Street, *Chicago* — 72
510 Madison, *New York* — 72
The Brooklyner, *New York* — 73
Cosmopolitan Resort & Casino, *Las Vegas* — 73
The Elysian, *Chicago* — 73
Met 2, *Miami* — 74
Residences at the Ritz-Carlton, *Philadelphia* — 74
Terminus 200, *Atlanta* — 74
Trump SoHo Hotel, *New York* — 75
Two Alliance Center, *Atlanta* — 75
W Hoboken, *Hoboken* — 75

Best Tall Building Asia & Australasia

Winner:
Pinnacle @ Duxton, *Singapore* — 78

Finalists:
iSQUARE, *Hong Kong* — 84
Marina Bay Sands, *Singapore* — 88
Nanjing Greenland Financial Center, *Nanjing* — 92
Northeast Asia Trade Tower, *Incheon* — 96

Nominees:
400 George Street, *Brisbane* — 100
BEA Financial Tower, *Shanghai* — 102
BUMPS, *Beijing* — 104
China Diamond Exchange Center, *Shanghai* — 106
Crown Hotel at City of Dreams, *Macau* — 107
Deloitte Centre, *Auckland* — 108
MOSAIC, *Beijing* — 110
NHN Green Factory, *Seongnam* — 111
Santos Place, *Brisbane* — 112
Songdo First World Towers, *Incheon* — 113
39 Conduit Road, *Hong Kong* — 114
City Square Residences, *Singapore* — 114
Kalpataru Towers, *Mumbai* — 114
Kwun Tong 223, *Hong Kong* — 115

The Masterpiece, *Hong Kong* 115
The St. Francis Shangri-la, *Mandaluyong City* 115

Best Tall Building Europe

Winner:
Broadcasting Place, *Leeds* 118

Finalists:
Hegau Tower, *Singen* 124
PalaisQuartier Office Tower, *Frankfurt* 128

Nominees:
Caja Madrid Tower, *Madrid* 132
Mosfilmovskaya, *Moscow* 134
Stadthaus, *London* 136
Strata SE1, *London* 138
Candle House, *Leeds* 140
Imperia Tower, *Moscow* 140
Maastoren, *Rotterdam* 140
The Mill and Jerwood Dance House, *Ipswich* 141
Opernturm, *Frankfurt* 141
Sea Towers, *Gdynia* 141

Best Tall Building Middle East & Africa

Winner:
Burj Khalifa, *Dubai* 144

Finalist:
O-14, *Dubai* 150

Nominees:
Al Bidda Tower, *Doha* 154
Al Tijaria Tower, *Kuwait City* 156
Arraya Office Tower, *Kuwait City* 158
Ocean Heights, *Dubai* 159
The Address, *Dubai* 160
Al Salam Tecom Tower, *Dubai* 160

Boulevard Plaza, *Dubai* 160
Nassima Tower, *Dubai* 161
Sama Tower, *Dubai* 161
Tiffany Tower, *Dubai* 161

Lifetime Achievement Awards

Lifetime Achievement Awards Criteria 162
Lynn S. Beedle Award, *William Pedersen* 164
Fazlur Khan Medal, *Ysrael A. Seinuk* 170
CTBUH 2010 Fellows 176

Awards & CTBUH Information

Awards Committee 2010 177
Review of Past Winners 178
Review of CTBUH 2009 Awards Dinner 180
CTBUH Height Criteria 184
Tallest 100 Buildings List 188

Index of Buildings 192
Index of Companies 193
Image Credits 196
CTBUH Organizational Structure & Members 198

On behalf of the CTBUH I would like to thank Ahmad Abdelrazaq, Bruce Kuwabara, Peter Murray, Matthias Schuler, Mun Summ Wong, and Antony Wood for joining me on this year's jury. This is the second year I've had the pleasure of acting as Jury Chair, and the deliberations always provoke a spirited and inspiring debate on what constitutes quality in design.

The Council's annual awards program continues to attract increasing interest from around the globe; the quality of the submissions received this year was extremely high. At 86, the number of entries also exceeded our expectations, and I'd like to specially thank Steven Henry, Publications Coordinator and CTBUH Awards program manager, and Peter Weismantle, my awards committee support within Smith + Gill, for their dedicated efforts to organize the awards process.

The winners of the CTBUH Awards represent the best completed tall buildings in the world each year. Projects are evaluated for ingenuity in design, quality of design execution and also against one another. In evaluating the entries, the quality of ideas, the implementation of detail, aesthetic, contextual approach and sustainability were all aspects of discussion.

The jury also considered other aspects that contributed to the project's success: its cultural significance, success in "placemaking" and how it excelled in related disciplines like structural engineering. These aspects are integral to the continuing advancement of practice and should be factored into any comprehensive discussion of great architecture.

In the 21st century, the need to advance these and other related aspects is critical, especially in supertall buildings. Global migration to urban areas has presented a true challenge to architects and planners, as we attempt to create comfortable, sustainable environments for increasingly dense cities. Innovation through programming, true sustainable design and calculated eco-density have now come to the forefront of discussion.

Is it possible to build truly sustainable supertall structures? Of course. In fact, supertall buildings offer tremendous advantages in the creation of sustainable cities. They immediately reduce claimed land use and require less infrastructure than neighboring low-rise buildings of the same total size. A 90-story building requires less land, less roadway and less urban infrastructure than three 30-story buildings. A supertall building can incorporate a mixed-use program to offer a live-work or vertical city experience.

Planned properly, these structures can densify urban centers in very sustainable ways. In addition, as technically advanced buildings with state-of the-art structures and MEP systems, they're designed for longer life spans than many other buildings, which add to their core sustainability.

Yet sustainability is also about more than just environmental awareness. We can't only measure it by kw/h and through using advanced MEP systems. While these elements are critical, sustainability is also about strengthening our economy, our education and our culture. At the highest level of design, issues of cultural and economic sustainability are integral to a building's success.

At a presentation at the Louvre in Paris last year, I was asked by an audience member what the value of sustainability was in a project that was supertall or the "World's Tallest." The person asking wondered if it would be better to build smaller buildings or culturally programmed buildings as opposed to mega structures. While it was a fair question, I found it ironic that it would be posed in Paris, the City of Lights, a city architecturally defined by The Eiffel Tower. What is the Eiffel Tower's program? Is it sustainable? Should it be there?

Certain projects serve primarily to bring cultural value to their cities and countries. They mark a moment in time, when people or rulers desired to establish their culture as globally significant and chose architecture as a means of broadcasting that message. For centuries, this has been the case: the Pyramids, Cathedrals, even Obelisks like the CN Tower or the Eiffel Tower have tremendous value in the identity of a place.

Today, we expect that energy savings, the reduction of embodied energy, and the incorporation of recycled materials are all integral to a project. But it is critical we remember that architecture is about the confluence of many factors; about the integration of art and science. Cultural sustainability has just as much value as energy reduction or lowering a building's carbon footprint. The projects CTBUH has honored this year exemplify this.

It has been an honor and pleasure to represent the CTBUH for the last two years. It is my hope and expectation that CTBUH will continue to define methods of excellence for practice, and that we, as practitioners, will measure our work against these high standards of distinction.

Gordon Gill
Awards Committee Chair 2009–2010
Adrian Smith + Gordon Gill Architecture
Chicago, USA

2010: An Overview

The year 2010 is the most successful year of skyscraper completion in the history of urban development to date, certainly in terms of both number of buildings and average height. Although there have been intense periods of tall building construction in specific geographic areas throughout history—late nineteenth century Chicago, art deco New York or post-second world war Europe for example—the boom of the past two decades has been unprecedented in that it has taken place across virtually the entire globe—from Toronto to Tokyo, Rio to Riyadh, Brisbane to Beijing.

The facts are staggering. Some 47 of the current 100 tallest buildings in the world have been completed in the past five years, since the end of 2005, with 23 of these buildings completed in just this year, 2010, alone. In addition, a further 33 buildings will enter the list in the next two years (see the CTBUH official 100 world's tallest buildings list, page 188). This will translate into a 67% change in the "100 World's Tallest" in just seven years, by the end of 2012.

At the "World's Tallest" end of the data, 2010 witnesses an incredible feat (see "History of the 'World's Tallest Building'" diagram opposite bottom). No previous tall building in history has surpassed its predecessor by more than 68m (221ft), but Burj Khalifa completing at 828m (2,717ft) this year achieves an unprecedented 320m (1,050ft) leap over the previous world's tallest, Taipei 101. This increase in overall height (see "Average height of the 100 tallest buildings" graph below) is also true of the average height of the "100 World's Tallest," which has more than doubled since 1930 and, increased by 15% in the decade 2000–2010 alone. 2007 marked the point where the average height of the 100 Tallest Buildings surpassed the 300 meter mark—the threshold for supertall.

In terms of supertall buildings (i.e., those in excess of 300 meters—or 984 feet—in height), there were only 13 supertall buildings in existence internationally in 1990. By the end of 2010 this number is expected to be 56; a 430% increase in just two decades. But it is not just at the supertall end that tall buildings have been proliferating. As our graph on all tall buildings greater than 200 meters shows (opposite top), the total number of buildings over 200 meters in existence around the world has more than doubled in the last ten years. This year alone, 106 buildings over 200 meters are expected to be completed.

Of course, it is not without considerable irony that 2010 is being heralded as the most successful year of skyscraper completion to date, given that much of the world is currently limping out of significant recession, with its eyes cast warily back towards a dreaded double-dip downturn. The buildings that we see completed now are clearly the product of market confidence and construction starts from 4–6 years ago, and this lag effect between start and completion casts an awkward schism between the necessary buzz word of the moment—austerity—and the perceived exuberance of shining tall towers hitting the market.

What is not completely apparent from these overall number statistics and perceived exuberance is that

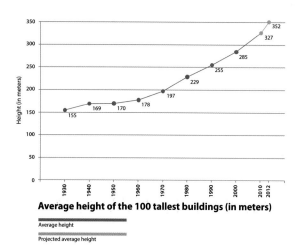

Average height of the 100 tallest buildings (in meters)

Average height

Projected average height

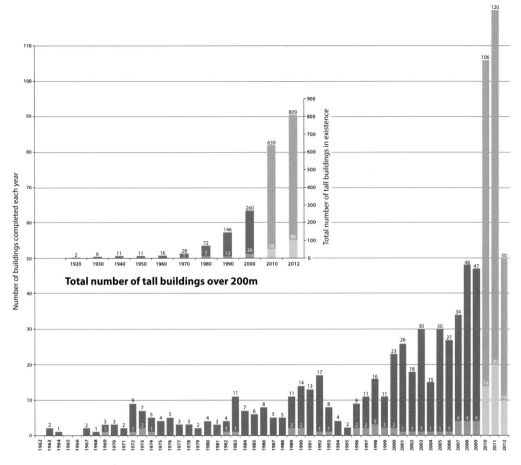

Number of buildings completed each year

Total number of tall buildings over 200m

Total number of tall buildings in existence

Tall buildings completed each year over 200m

Number of 200m+ buildings

Number of supertalls (300m+)

Projected number of 200m+ buildings

Projected number of supertalls (300m+)

Notes:
1. We can predict 2010–2012 building completions with some accuracy due to projects now in advanced construction. From 2012, we expect to see a drop in the number of tall buildings completed due to the global recession, until the worldwide economy recovers.
2. Totals after 2001 take into account the destruction of the World Trade Center Towers 1 and 2.

History of the "World's Tallest Building"

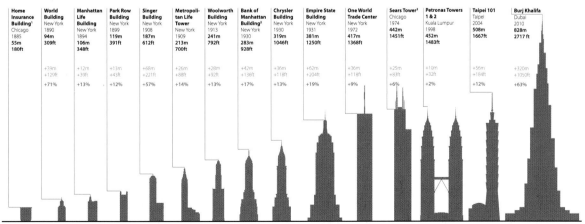

[1]While the Home Insurance Building was never the tallest building in the world, it is considered the first skyscraper constructed (framed/non-loadbearing façade construction) and thus the first "tall building" as defined by the CTBUH.

[2]Now known as The Trump Building, "Bank of Manhattan Building" was the building's title when it was the "World's Tallest Building"

[3]Now known as Willis Tower, "Sears Tower" was the building's title when it was the "World's Tallest Building"

the world of tall buildings has changed fundamentally over the past decade or two, with a number of trends now evident. These trends are in addition to the simple trends of more—and taller—tall buildings being constructed and demonstrate fundamental shifts in predominant location, function and materials (illustrated in the graphs opposite).

The first of these trends, now commonly acknowledged and borne out in the decade comparative statistics (see location graph opposite top) is that the predominant location of the tallest buildings has been changing rapidly. Whereas as recently as 1990, 80% of the "100 World's Tallest" were located in North America, now that figure is only 27%, with the shift occurring predominantly to Asia (45%, with 34% in China alone), and the Middle East (24%, with 17% in Dubai alone). By the end of 2012, the number of the world's tallest 100 buildings in North America is expected to be only 18%, with 43% in Asia and 33% in the Middle East.

Perhaps more interesting than the number, height, and location statistics, is how the function and structural material of the tallest buildings has been changing, with major moves away from the steel office buildings which have dominated the tallest lists for many decades. We are now seeing residential and mixed-use functions influence the list, up to 38% from 12% in just the last decade, whilst single steel buildings have dropped from 38% to 23% in favor of concrete and composite structure over the last decade, and from 90% as recently as 1970.

There are a number of reasons for all these changes, not least in the motivations driving these buildings in the first place. Whereas tall buildings have often been used as marketing tools to portray the vitality of a corporation, now they are increasingly being used to portray the vitality of a city or country on a competitive world stage. This is reflected in the titles of the buildings themselves—previously endowed with names such as Woolworth, Sears, Petronas, they are now more likely to be named Burj Dubai, Chicago Spire, Shanghai Tower. The buildings are being used to brand a city, since many cities, especially in developing countries, believe it necessary to have a signature skyline to be considered successful and thriving.

There are other reasons for this increase in tall buildings in the East. It is believed that there are almost 200,000 people urbanizing on this planet every day (United Nations statistics), requiring a new city of about one million inhabitants every week to cope with this migration from rural to urban. But, happening predominantly in developing countries with large populations such as China, India, Brazil and Indonesia, these people are not flocking to new cities, but rather to existing cities, putting significant strain on existing urban space and infrastructure. Be it new or existing cities, the question of how these new urban inhabitants are accommodated is a challenging one. It is increasingly being seen that the American model of a dense downtown working core with a massive, ever-expanding suburb is an unsustainable one, due to the increased infrastructure needed (roads, power, lighting, waste handling, etc), as well as the energy expenditure and carbon emission implications of the home-work commute. Thus it is increasingly being recognized that cities need to become denser to create more sustainable patterns of life—to reduce the horizontal spread of infrastructure networks needed to support, and to be more efficient in land use, partly for retention of "natural" land for agricultural purposes.

Though tall buildings are not the only solution to achieving high density in cities, they can be part of the solution. This, coupled with the city-symbolism/iconic factor, has certainly been influential in the escalation of the number of tall buildings being built and planned

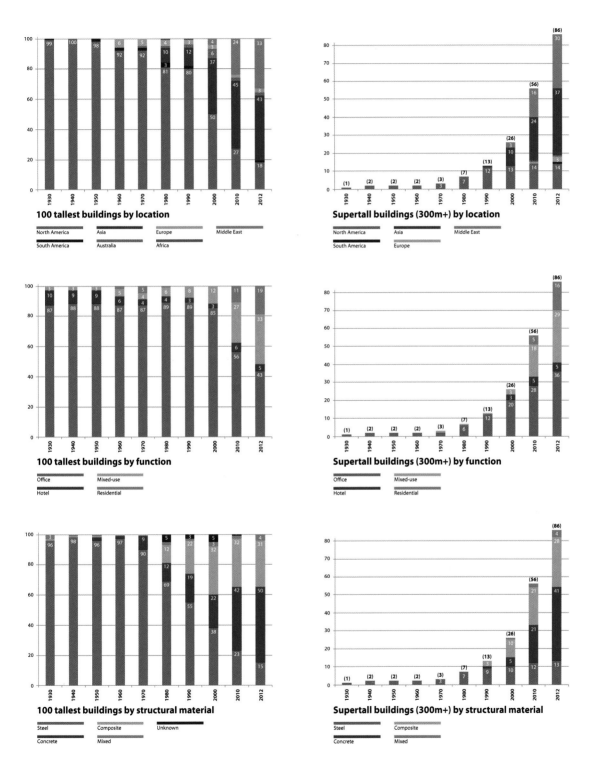

100 tallest buildings by location

North America Asia Europe Middle East
South America Australia Africa

Supertall buildings (300m+) by location

North America Asia Middle East
South America Europe

100 tallest buildings by function

Office Mixed-use
Hotel Residential

Supertall buildings (300m+) by function

Office Mixed-use
Hotel Residential

100 tallest buildings by structural material

Steel Composite Unknown
Concrete Mixed

Supertall buildings (300m+) by structural material

Steel Composite
Concrete Mixed

Note: All 2010 and 2012 figures are projections to end of year data. See Height Criteria (pages 184–187) for all definitions

in developing countries. It perhaps also partially explains why many of these buildings are residential in nature rather than commercial—to accommodate the growing populace in the city.

There are other reasons for the shift to residential and mixed-use however, not least the commercial incentive to "edge bets" on fluctuating demand for office–residential–hotel functions by including all in the building program. It also makes sense that, if the objective of great height is a predominant one, then it is easier to achieve this with a residential rather than an office function. Residential floor plates tend to be much smaller than office ones—an advantage when subjecting materials to wind and other pressures almost a kilometer in the sky—and also require less floor-area-consuming elevators and other vertical services to support the function. In other words, if the creation of the "World's Tallest Building" is the primary motivator, then it is easier to do it with a function that will put less people in continual occupation at the top of the tower and thus reduce the size of the floors to house them and services to support them.

The reasons for the trend towards concrete/composite structure in the world's tallest buildings are similarly multi-layered. This is partly a product of the developing countries where these projects are located—which are much more likely to have sufficient concrete technological expertise, over steel. The aforementioned change towards residential and mixed-use functions is also influential, since the fire, acoustic and cellular requirements of living lend themselves better to concrete construction rather than open-plan-enabling steel. There are also many who believe that the increased performance required of the structure at great height—through the required damping of movement as well as the transfer of vertical loads—can be more adequately handled by steel and concrete acting together compositely, rather than one material alone.

CTBUH 2010 Awards

So how have the trends given in this opening statistical overview affected the projects submitted this year for the CTBUH 2010 awards—the projects that are profiled in the pages of this book? Well, in addition to the "World's Tallest Building"—the Burj Khalifa (page 144) evidencing all the trends very neatly (i.e., it is supertall, located in a "developing" country, of mixed-use function and a predominantly concrete structure) it is interesting to note that, of the 86 projects we had submitted for this year's awards (incidentally, up from 54 submitted buildings last year), 66% are of residential, mixed-use or hotel function, and 66% are constructed of concrete or composite structure.

However, of course, the CTBUH annual awards are not about numbers or statistics, they are about quality of design and execution. In the introduction to last year's

Best Tall Buildings Americas
Opposite: Winner, Bank of America Tower, New York
Top Left: Finalist, Aqua Tower, Chicago
Bottom Left: Finalist, Veer Towers, Las Vegas
Right: Finalist, One Madison Park, New York

2009 Awards Book, whilst generally being upbeat about the improving quality of the buildings submitted and awards program overall, I bemoaned the fact that the Americas and Middle East & Africa regions seemed to be, on average, far behind Asia & Australasia and Europe in terms of ambition and achievement generally, and sustainable performance specifically. Although there were numerous projects in both these regional categories that exhibited many of those qualities, it seemed that, especially in North America, the nominations were generally more commercially-driven, with many elegantly-designed, glass, rectilinear boxes that provided good, efficient usable floor area returns for the developer, but didn't necessarily advance the typology of tall buildings beyond what has been typical in the western hemisphere for numerous decades.

In can be nothing more than a happy coincidence of course, but in one short year I am happy to report that the quality of completed tall buildings in both the Americas and Middle East regions has, in my view, risen dramatically. Last year we recognized only one winner and one finalist in the Americas region, whereas this year we have one winner and three finalists. Although Bank of America Tower, New York, has deservedly taken the Americas title with its angular form, positive relationship to site and commitment to reducing energy consumption (page 22), in another year each of the other three finalists could quite easily have taken the title, from the curving gracefulness of Chicago's Aqua tower (page 28), to the cantilevered glass boxes of One Madison Park (page 32), to the exquisitely detailed façade of Veer Towers (page 36). It is also important to note that, whereas the Americas

Best Tall Buildings Middle East & Africa
Left: Winner, Burj Khalifa, Dubai
Right: Finalist, O-14, Dubai

region is still dominated by entries from the north of the continent (the USA home of the CTBUH obviously having an influence on submissions there), four entries from the Americas are from outside the USA and Canada this year, as opposed to just one last year. It is great to see Brazil, Chile and Mexico represented within the Americas region—a trend that, given the significant tall building work being developed in those countries, is set to continue in the coming years.

The Middle East tells a similar story this year. Whilst rightly dominated by the architectural and engineering marvel that is the Burj Khalifa, it is likely that the refreshing aesthetics of the finalist O-14 building (page 150) would have given the project the title of "Best" in most other years. O-14 reflects the positive moves towards more variation in material, form and expression that is occurring in tall buildings. Though many will think that the success of the Burj Khalifa as "Best Tall Building" for this region was a given, I can report that the debate amongst the jury between these two was not as clear cut as many would have thought.

Despite the positive steps forward in the Americas and Middle East, I still believe that the Europe and Asia & Australasia regions are producing more interesting and sustainable tall buildings on average. The seven-linked towers of the Asia & Australasia winner, the Pinnacle at Duxton, Singapore, scheme (page 78), with public communal areas stretched between and around the towers at ground, 26th and 50th floors, would be an incredible achievement in any city. The fact that this is essentially government-built social housing makes the achievement all the more remarkable.

The idea of sky bridges is clearly taking on in a big way in Singapore, with finalist Marina Bay Sands completing three splaying hotel towers linked with one huge, cantilevering external sky deck at the roof plane (page 88). The other finalists in the Asia & Australasia region—the retail revolution that is the 28-story shopping mall, iSQUARE (page 84), the Nanjing Greenland Financial Center (page 92), and the twisting Northeast Asia Trade Tower at Songdo (pages 96), really show the vibrancy of the Asia region overall.

Best Tall Buildings Asia & Australasia
Top Left: Winner, Pinnacle @ Duxton, Singapore
Middle Left: Finalist, Marina Bay Sands, Singapore
Bottom Left: Finalist, Northeast Asia Trade Tower, Incheon
Top Right: Finalist, iSQUARE, Hong Kong
Bottom Right: Finalist, Nanjing Greenland Financial Center, Nanjing

The achievements on the European scene are more subtle than the theatrics of some of the Asian projects, but are none the less impressive. The changing angular geometry and shear gusto of cladding on the European winner, Broadcasting Place, Leeds, in cor-ten (page 118) simply blew the jury away during deliberations. Also impressive were the juxtaposition of angular forms at the finalist PalaisQuartier Office Tower (page 128) and the exquisite handling of glass façade at finalist Hegau Tower (page 124). Underpinning many of the European towers was a commitment to energy/carbon reduction—sometimes in material usage as well as operation—that is perhaps indication that we are moving beyond the "sustainable technology as trophy" aesthetic in this region more than in others.

The Immediate Future

Now, perhaps on to the question that is on many people's lips: 2010 may have been a great year in number, height and quality of tall buildings, but what of the future? How has the global recession affected the typology and what can we expect to see being completed—or even built—in a few short years from now? Well, though of course you would naturally expect me to be upbeat about tall buildings, there are also a number of solid indicators we can draw on. The first is that, contrary to many beliefs only a decade or two ago, and certainly in the immediate aftermath of 9/11, we can say with some certainty that the tall building as a viable proposition for our cities is now ensured. The contribution to higher urban densities as a response to climate change and more sustainable patterns of life have elevated the typology beyond what many saw as only vanity (be it corporate or governmental) a few short years ago, to the point where many now consider them necessary. Although, for sure, they are nowhere near their fullest potential of sustainable evolution, tall buildings can, and will, contribute to more sustainable cities. For this reason alone, they will be considered as increasingly viable building types in the future.

Without doubt there will be a short-term decline in the number of skyscrapers being completed each year in a few years from now as a consequence of the decline in construction starts through the impact of the recession now. However, as the projected figures for 2011–2012 in the graphs illustrated earlier show (see page 9), the amazing trends towards the numbers and height of the past decade are set to continue in skyscraper completion at least for the next two years, with 2011 likely to surpass 2010 as the most successful year of skyscraper completion ever, despite the global recession. CTBUH statistics show that there are currently more than 320 buildings over 200 meters actively in construction around the world.

Presuming that most of these will proceed to completion, and given that other projects are starting all the time, that should ensure a healthy number of completions globally, even in the leaner years ahead. For anyone that doubts this, the daily-updated CTBUH Global News section on our website highlights the tall building projects around the world that are announced

Best Tall Buildings Europe
Opposite: Winner, Broadcasting Place, Leeds
Left: Finalist, PalaisQuartier Office Tower, Frankfurt
Right: Finalist, Hegua Tower, Singen

almost daily. And, though it may surprise many, there is still hardly a week that goes by without some supertall project, or the world's "next tallest," flashing across our desks here at CTBUH. Though many of these projects will not move beyond the fanciful or cynical marketing exercise, it shows that there is still a high level of interest in creating tall buildings around the world.

As to the other changes—in location, function, and structural material—all the indicators are that those trends will continue into the near future, and probably intensify. The greatest change that needs to happen, however, is the move towards more sustainable tall buildings in construction and operation (and demolition/dismantling/re-use). We need to work out how to do more with less, and create tall buildings that are more intrinsically inspired by—and plugged into—their locale; physically, environmentally, and culturally. Considering the tall building not as a monolithic sculpture but as a series of communities (be it of single or varying functions), where each

horizon within a common framework would have a different opportunity to relate to both city and climate would be a good place to start, as would the vision to justify every expenditure of carbon/material provision by giving all elements multiple—rather than single—functions. As I look through the pages of this book I see many of these things starting to happen, though it's happening too slowly for some. Time will tell if the tall building will ever reach a completely satisfactory state of evolution in both energy and cultural terms but, as the global recession puts paid to some of the more excessive tall ideas of the past decade, I genuinely believe it's heading in the right direction. My congratulations to all the award winners, finalists, nominees and our Lifetime Achievement winners, Bill Pedersen and Ysrael Seinuk, profiled in this book.

Antony Wood
Editor
CTBUH Executive Director
Chicago, USA
July 2010

Best Tall Building
Awards Criteria

The Council on Tall Buildings and Urban Habitat initiated its Awards Program in 2001, with the creation of the Lynn S. Beedle Lifetime Achievement Award. It began recognizing the team achievement in tall building projects by issuing Best Tall Building Awards in 2007, to give recognition to projects that have made extraordinary contributions to the advancement of tall buildings and the urban environment, and that achieve sustainability at the highest and broadest level. It issues four regional awards each year (Americas, Asia & Australasia, Europe and Middle East & Africa). In addition, from the four "regional" awards, one project is awarded the honor of "Best Tall Building Overall" which is announced on the night of the awards ceremony.

The winning projects must exhibit processes and/or innovations that have added to the profession of design and enhance cities and the lives of their inhabitants. Criteria for submission includes:

1) The project must be completed (topped out architecturally, fully clad, and at least partially occupied) no earlier than the 1st of January of the previous year, and no later than the 1st of October of the current awards year (e.g., for the 2010 Awards, a project must have a completion date between January 1, 2009 and October 1, 2010).

2) The project advances seamless integration of architectural form, structure, building systems, sustainable design strategies, and life safety for its occupants.

3) The project exhibits sustainable qualities at a broad level:
Environment: Minimize effects on the natural environment through proper site utilization, innovative uses of materials, energy reduction, use of alternative energy sources, reduced emissions and water consumption.
People: Must have a positive effect on the inhabitants and the quality of human life.
Community: Must demonstrate relevance to the contemporary and future needs of the community in which it is located.
Economic: The building should add economic vitality to its occupants, owner, and community

4) The project must achieve a high standard of excellence and quality in its realization.

5) The site planning and response to its immediate context must ensure rich and meaningful urban environments.

6) The contributions of the project should be generally consistent with the values and mission of the CTBUH.

Note: Awards in some categories may not be conferred on an annual basis if the criteria cannot be clearly met or demonstrated through the submittal.

Opposite: 2010 Winners, from left to right: Bank of America Tower, New York (Americas); Pinnacle @ Duxton, Singapore (Asia & Australasia); Broadcasting Place, Leeds (Europe); Burj Khalifa, Dubai (Middle East & Africa)

Best Tall Building
Americas

The Bank of America Tower

New York, USA

The Bank of America Tower at One Bryant Park was designed to set a new standard in high-performance buildings, for both the office workers who occupy the tower and for a city and country that are awakening to the modern imperative of sustainability. Drawing on concepts of biophilia—or humans' innate need for connection to the natural environment—the vision at the occupant scale was to create the highest quality modern workplace by emphasizing daylight, fresh air, and an intrinsic connection to the outdoors. At the urban scale, the tower addresses its local environment as well as the context of midtown Manhattan, to which it adds an expressive new silhouette on an already-iconic skyline.

The building responds to the dense urban context by weaving into the existing grid at street level, yet challenging the boundaries of public and private space with a highly transparent corner entry. As it rises, the tower shears into two offset halves, increasing the verticality of its proportions as well as the surface area exposed to daylight. Mass is sliced from these two rectilinear volumes, producing angular facets that open up light and oblique views beyond the typical limits of urban geometry. The crystalline form—inspired by the legacy of the 1853 Crystal Palace, which once stood adjacent in Bryant Park, and by a quartz crystal from the client's collection—suggests an appropriate natural analogue, both organic and urban in nature. With its crisp, folded façade, the tower changes with the sun and sky; its southeast exposure, a deep double wall, orients the building in its full height toward Bryant Park, its namesake and the most intensively-used open space in the US.

With the Bank of America as its primary tenant, occupying six trading floors and 75% of its interior, the tower signals a significant shift in corporate America and in the real estate industry, acknowledging the higher value of healthy, productive workplaces. One Bryant Park's most lasting achievement is to merge the ethics of the green building movement with a twenty-first century aesthetic of transparency and re-connection.

One Bryant Park is the first commercial high-rise to earn LEED Platinum certification from the US Green Building Council. The building's advanced technologies include a clean-burning, on-site, 5.0 MW cogeneration plant, which provides approximately 65% of the building's annual electricity requirements and lowers daytime peak demand by 30%. A thermal storage system further helps reduce peak load on the city's over-taxed electrical grid by producing ice at night, melted during the day to provide cooling. Nearly all of the 1.2m (4ft) of annual rain and snow that fall on the site is captured and re-used as gray water to flush toilets and supply the cooling towers.

Completion Date: May 2010
Height to Architectural Top[1]: 366m (1,200ft)
Stories[1]: 55
Area: 115,000 sq m (1,237,850 sq ft)
Primary Use[1]: Office
Owner: Durst Organization; The Bank of America
Developer: Durst Organization
Design Architect: Cook+Fox Architects LLP
Associate Architect: Adamson Associates
Structural Engineer: Severud Associates Consulting Engineers
MEP Engineer: Jaros, Baum & Bolles Consulting Engineers
Main Contractor: Tishman Construction

[1] For all definitions used in the data sections throughout this book, refer to CTBUH criteria shown on pages 184–187

Opposite: Overall view of the building and Bryant Park from the south east

"An excellent example of attention to detail, commitment to sustainability, placing priority on human health and pushing boundaries in environmental strategies and technology."

Gordon Gill, Awards Chair, Adrian Smith + Gordon Gill Architecture

> "The architects have made much of the quality of life for those occupying the building and the angular form delivers internal spaces of great variety without sacrificing an efficient and functional building."
>
> *Peter Murray, Juror, New London Architecture Centre*

These strategies, along with waterless urinals and low-flow fixtures, save approximately 7.7 million gallons of potable water per year.

Recycling was a prominent factor throughout the building's construction, with 91% of construction and demolition waste diverted from landfill. Materials include steel made from 75% (minimum) recycled content and concrete made from cement containing 45% recycled content (blast furnace slag). To protect indoor air quality as well as natural resources, interior materials are low-VOC, sustainably harvested, manufactured locally, and/or recycled wherever possible. The building's exceptionally high indoor environmental quality results from hospital-grade, 95% filtered air;

abundant natural daylight and 2.9m (9.5ft) ceilings; an under-floor ventilation system with individually-controlled floor diffusers; round-the-clock air quality monitoring; and views through a clear, floor-to-ceiling glass curtain wall. This high-performance curtain wall minimizes solar heat gain through low-E glass and heat-reflecting ceramic frit; it also has allowed the Bank of America to reduce artificial lighting with an automated daylight dimming system, reducing lighting and cooling energy by up to 10%.

On an urban level, the project also represents the culmination of the developer's multigenerational efforts to revitalize the Times Square area, and gives back to the city with a street-level Urban Garden

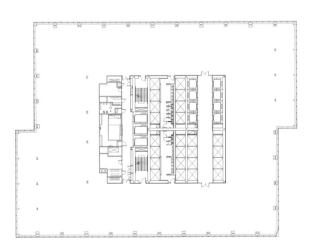

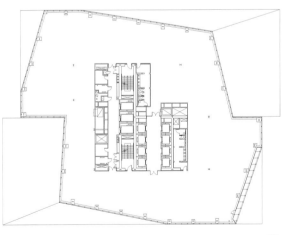

Jury Statement

The Bank of America Tower produces a high level of sustainability within the commercial market place, creating a strong identity for itself and acting as an exemplary execution of sustainable technology integration, urban intensification, and advanced workplace design on the most broad levels. With its chamfered top and crystalline geometry, the form of the building eschews the orthogonal blocks of the Modernist tradition creating a sculptural addition to the New York skyline without sacrificing the efficiency and functionality of the office floor plans.

It is admirable to see a tall building design that is so thoroughly focused on the end user, creating a high quality work space with emphasis on daylight, fresh air, and a healthy work environment. There is little doubt that this balanced and sustainable design will be used as a benchmark for future sustainable and well integrated projects worldwide.

Room, a mid-block pedestrian passage/performance space, and the first "green" Broadway theater, the LEED Gold Stephen Sondheim Theater.

In an era of heightened security, a central challenge of the project was balancing the complexities of program and scale with high-performance architecture and urban design. In its layered connection to the ground plane, One Bryant Park resolves this question with a progression of public and private spaces—from Bryant Park to the Urban Garden Room to the semi-public lobby. As a total response to the urban environment, the building's restorative connections therefore work on many levels, from green roofs and views of the park to more subtle and expressive elements. A highly integrated approach to architecture and engineering ensured a close relationship between form and function. Bridging contexts as vastly different as Times Square and Bryant Park, the project makes a highly visible statement on urban stewardship and global citizenship for the 21st century.

Top Left: The ground floor Urban Garden Room, a public space
Bottom Left: The building entry, subway connection and canopy
Opposite: Building sections showing air conditioning and water handling

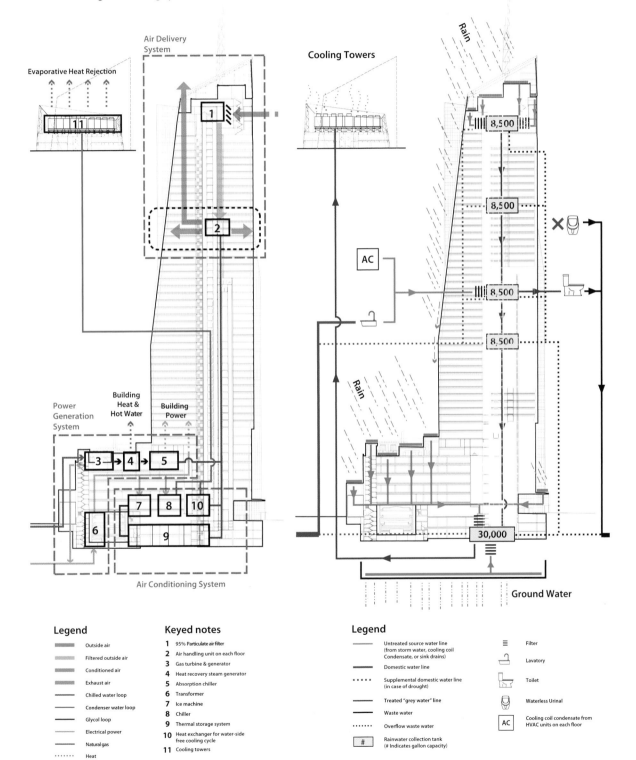

Section showing air handling systems

Evaporative Heat Rejection

Air Delivery System

11

1

2

Power Generation System

Building Heat & Hot Water

Building Power

3 → **4** → **5**

7 | **8** | **10**

6 | **9**

Air Conditioning System

Legend

	Outside air
	Filtered outside air
	Conditioned air
	Exhaust air
	Chilled water loop
	Condenser water loop
	Glycol loop
	Electrical power
	Natural gas
	Heat

Keyed notes

1 95% Particulate air filter
2 Air handling unit on each floor
3 Gas turbine & generator
4 Heat recovery steam generator
5 Absorption chiller
6 Transformer
7 Ice machine
8 Chiller
9 Thermal storage system
10 Heat exchanger for water-side free cooling cycle
11 Cooling towers

Section showing water handling systems

Rain

Cooling Towers

8,500

8,500

AC

8,500

8,500

Rain

30,000

Ground Water

Legend

	Untreated source water line (from storm water, cooling coil Condensate, or sink drains)
	Domestic water line
	Supplemental domestic water line (in case of drought)
	Treated "grey water" line
	Waste water
	Overflow waste water
#	Rainwater collection tank (# Indicates gallon capacity)

≡	Filter
	Lavatory
	Toilet
	Waterless Urinal
AC	Cooling coil condensate from HVAC units on each floor

Aqua Tower

Chicago, USA

Unlike a tower in an open field, new towers in urban environments must negotiate small viewing corridors between existing buildings. In response to this, the Aqua Tower is designed to capture particular views that would otherwise be unattainable. A series of contours defined by outdoor terraces extends away from the face of the tower structure to provide views between neighboring buildings. The terraces inflect based on criteria such as the view, solar shading and size and type of dwelling. When viewed together, these unique terraces make the building appear to undulate, presenting a highly sculptural appearance that is rooted in function.

These outdoor terraces are cantilevered up to 4m (12ft) and have a depth of 23cm (9in) which thins out towards the edge of the cantilever to assist with water drainage. The terraces differ in shape from floor to floor causing each floor plate to differ. The challenge of constructing unique floor plates was solved by implementing a computerized civil engineering and surveying software program and digital CAD files for inputting the coordinates of each unique slab to a robotic station used onsite. This system was used to set in place light-gauge steel plate edge-forms according to the contours. After the concrete had set, these steel forms would be removed and easily reshaped according to the contours of the next level.

Among the building's notable features is the green roof terrace atop its plinth—which at 7,000 sq m (75,350 sq ft) is one of Chicago's largest. It contains an outdoor pool, running track, gardens, fire pits and a yoga terrace. From below, Aqua's plinth navigates the site's complexity by spanning over pre-existing elements, such as an electrical substation, and by aligning with existing infrastructure, including an adjacent three-level roadway. The plinth physically connects pedestrian areas with stairs and elevators linking street level to park level and the lakefront.

The tower's east–west orientation maximizes its winter solar performance. Its balconies extend further on the southern façade to provide shading, reducing solar exposure in summer and allowing passive warming in winter. In addition to low-E coatings on all glass, the design team modeled seasonal sun patterns to identify remaining areas of glass that needed higher performing glazing to increase energy efficiency throughout the tower. Glass on the east and south façades are reflective in areas without a protective balcony, while glass facing west has a tinted coating that improves its shading coefficient. In total, Aqua employs six different types of glass: clear, tinted, reflective, spandrel, fritted and translucent, the placement of which is determined by the orientation and function of interior space. Fritted glass is used and combined with handrail design to minimize bird strikes.

Completion Date: October 2009
Height to Architectural Top[1]**:** 262m (859ft)
Stories[1]**:** 86
Area: 184,936 sq m (1,990,634 sq ft)
Primary Use[1]**:** Mixed: Residential/Hotel
Owner/Developer: Magellan Development Group
Design Architect: Studio Gang Architects, Ltd
Associate Architect: Loewenberg Architects, LLC
Structural Engineer: Magnusson Klemencic Associates
MEP Engineer: Advanced Mechanical Systems, Inc; Gurtz Electric Company; Abbott Industries, Inc
Main Contractor: McHugh Construction
Other Consultants: IE Consultants, Inc; Khatib and Associates; McDaniel Fire System; Wolff Landscape Architecture, Inc; Ground Engineering Consultants, Inc; Case Foundation; Prairie Material Services, Inc; Schaaf Glass Co; EFCO Corp.

Opposite: Overall view from the north west

"To stand under Aqua and look up is to reveal an organic, sinuous view that does not exist anywhere else in the tall building world."

Antony Wood, Juror, CTBUH

Left: View looking up
Opposite Top Left: Overall view from east
Opposite Top Right: A community created on the tower's façade
Opposite Bottom Left: East–west section
Opposite Bottom Right: Typical floor plan

> "The differential cantilevering balconies on Aqua transform a standardized glass box into a sublime amorphous form."
>
> *Mun Summ Wong, Juror, WOHA Architects*

The building is also constructed on a former brownfield site, and 50% of its site is dedicated green open space, exceeding Chicago's standard zoning ordinance by 25%. This green roof is one of the largest in the city and also features a drainage system that includes water collection for its irrigation. Furthermore, Aqua exceeds the City of Chicago's minimal requirements for natural ventilation and sunlight by more than 50% in over 90% of its spaces.

Detailed wind tunnel studies were completed to confirm the performance of the structure under high winds. Initially, it was thought that a supplemental tuned mass damping system may be required to appropriately manage the effects of the wind on occupant comfort. However, during the testing, it was discovered that the undulating slab edges disrupted or "confused" the flow of wind around the tower, effectively reducing the wind demands, and this, combined with the effectiveness of the structural design, eliminated the need for a supplemental damping system.

Jury Statement

Though the thermal bridging characteristics are potentially problematic, Aqua Tower's signature cantilevered balconies are breathtaking; it is exemplary of where concrete technology can take tall building design today. When viewed as a whole, the balconies create a seemingly organic and free "motion" across the tower's façades unlike anything before seen in tall building design, and yet they are carefully planned to provide solar shading, views, and to correspond to the units within.

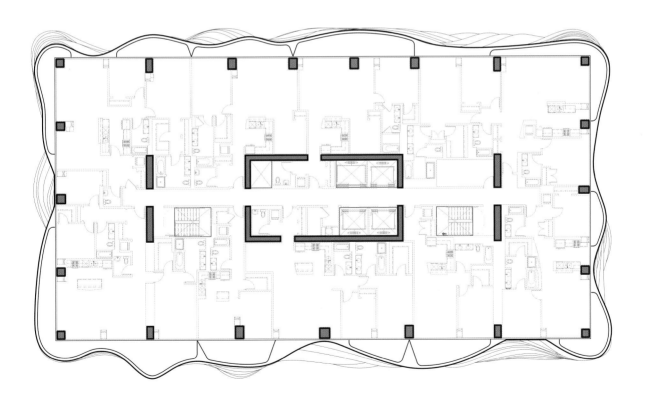

One Madison Park

New York, USA

One Madison Park is situated in a unique location on the Manhattan grid, fronting on East 23rd Street, a busy cross town thoroughfare—and at the foot of Madison Avenue, a major north–south thoroughfare that begins at 23rd Street, directly to the north. The tower acts as an axial icon on Madison Avenue, making the tower visible from great distances at the street level. The architectural challenge was to create a modern form that was respectful to the context of the Madison Square Park neighborhood while creating a visual dialogue with the adjacent historical high-rise building such as the Flatiron Building (1902) and the facing Met Life Tower (1909).

In order to allow construction to begin before the site could be entirely cleared it was decided that a portion of the tower would have to cantilever over an existing three-story building adjacent to the tower on its eastern side. The design team seized upon this idea to give the tower its unique configuration. From the main square mast of the tower clad in dark bronze glass, another shaft clad in white and clear glass is partially inserted and cantilevered from the main shaft in blocks ranging from four to six stories. The spaces between these blocks allowed for full floor residences with terraces built out onto the roof of the block below, that wrap around the north and east sides of the apartment.

The tower sits on a five-story base that holds commercial and service uses on the ground floor. Above the first floor, the base incorporates the main mechanical spaces and two levels of amenity spaces for the residents, which includes a fitness center, indoor pool, spa, and a private lounge with a terrace overlooking Madison Park.

Due to the placement of the tower in the middle of the site, each side could have windows opening to expansive views. Lateral bracing usually located around the perimeter was instead placed in the center, forming a cruciform of shear walls, buried between rooms and shafts minimizing the impact to room layouts. This integration of efficient space planning and structure gives each room within the homes an open expansive feeling focused on the city views beyond. High efficiency glazing was incorporated into the exterior skin to reduce solar heat gain with automated solar shading in each living room. An abundance of natural light is brought into every space of the tower which helps to minimize the need for artificial lighting. Due to its perimeter location, even the elevator lobby on every floor has a south facing window to bring in light and views.

The building's footprint is 15.25m x 16.15m (50ft x 53ft), which with its overall height of 189m (621ft) makes the tower one of the most slender buildings

Completion Date: June 2010
Height to Architectural Top[1]: 189m (621ft)
Stories[1]: 50
Area: 16,763 sq m (180,435 sq ft)
Primary Use[1]: Residential
Owner/Developer: Slazer Enterprises
Design Architect: CetraRuddy
Associate Architect: Cetra/CRI Architecture PLLC
Structural Engineer: WSP Cantor Seinuk
MEP Engineer: MG Engineering
Main Contractor: Bovis Lend Lease
Other Consultants: Israel Berger & Associates; Alan G. Davenport Wind Engineering Group; Van Deusen & Associates

Opposite: View from east

"Simply a unique and elegant solution derived without relying on excessive form making to create an 'identity' for itself."

Gordon Gill, Awards Chair, Adrian Smith + Gordon Gill Architecture

in New York with a height-to-width ratio of 12:1. Therefore, the lateral wind and seismic force-resisting system was the major engineering challenge. Naturally the shear wall stiffness and strength had to be maximized for this slender building while supporting the architectural design. This has been achieved by a combination of optimizing the configuration of the shear walls and using high performance concrete.

Due to its high slenderness ratio, the building's lateral dynamic movement is mitigated by the design and the incorporation of a Tuned Liquid Damping System to reduce the acceleration of building motions. The system is comprised of three cast-in-place reinforced concrete tanks filled with water and incorporated into the building structure at roof level. More specifically the tanks are known as Tuned Liquid Column Dampers which are U-shaped to maximize their effect while occupying less floor area. The dampers were designed to provide approximately 3% additional damping to the building, and reduce the building accelerations to acceptable levels.

Jury Statement

The strong yet simple form of One Madison Park rises from a seemingly impossibly small New York City site, presenting an elegant infill solution for increasing density in our land-constricted cities. The well integrated tower compliments its highly iconic, historic neighbors—Met Life Tower and Flatiron Building. Of similar height and proportion to the Met Life Tower, though strikingly different in appearance, these two towers—built over 100 years apart—play off one another and create an intriguing relationship.

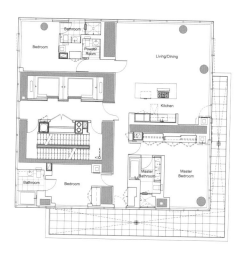

Veer Towers

Las Vegas, USA

Part of the new CityCenter complex in Las Vegas, Veer Towers attempts to blur the boundaries between the public and private realm while finding the right balance between becoming an integral part of the city while also giving the buildings and spaces a unique and iconic character. In approaching the design of the towers, the context was not a historical background to build upon, but the framework to establish a new order and create a new image. The Veer Towers lean at five degrees in opposite directions creating an architecture that is at once robust and delicate.

There's no reflective glass used on the project, making Veer the first truly transparent building in Las Vegas. Extensive use of high performance low-E coating glazing maximizes the introduction of day lighting and views to the outside, which in conjunction with the use of exterior shades and a 57% ceramic frit in 50% of the building's envelope, provide all the shading to control and reduce the solar loads. Staggered panels of clear and fritted yellow glass animate the façades and give the complex a welcome shot of color while horizontal louvers add a depth and texture to the exterior as well as provide shade from the intense desert sun.

The load-bearing structure is a simple and repetitive system with a Z-shaped central core. The cores of both towers are strategically positioned on the building's footprint in order to minimize gravity overturning effects, and they continue vertically up the entire building height. While all interior columns rise straight vertically, the tower columns on the north and south building elevations are inclined to follow the lean of the towers.

The south façade of the main building lobbies are expressed with slender concrete columns free standing at over 24m (80ft) high and inclined to articulate the lean of the towers. Due to space constraints and the requirement to maximize usable lobby space, composite column construction was introduced. The architectural design of the main lobby required a unique solution to the heating, cooling and ventilation due to the distinctive nature of these spaces. Each lobby is a multi-level space with a large expanse of glass on the south façade which runs the full height of the space. It provides large quantities of natural light to the lobby and large solar heat gains in summer and heat losses in winter. After studying the space loads and using computational fluid dynamics (CFD) analysis it was determined that the best solution for conditioning the space efficiently was a radiant floor system using chilled and heated water with displacement ventilation providing the required outside air ventilation and supplemental cooling/heating. A radiant cooling

Completion Date: March 2010
Height to Architectural Top[1]: 137m (449ft)
Stories[1]: 37
Area: 77,850 sq m (837,970 sq ft)
Primary Use[1]: Residential
Owner: MGM Mirage Design Group
Developer: MGM Mirage Design Group; Dubai World
Design Architect: Murphy/Jahn Architects
Associate Architect: Adamson Associates
Structural Engineer: Halcrow Yolles
MEP Engineer: WSP Flack + Kurtz
Main Contractor: Perini & Tishman Construction
Other Consultants: Werner Sobek Ingenieure; Israel Berger & Associates; ALT Cladding; AIK Expeditions Lumiere; L-Plan Lichtplanung; Lerch Bates & Associates

Opposite: Overall view from south east

"The use of color, the relative lean of the buildings and the exquisitely detailed façade give these towers a powerful dynamism."

Antony Wood, Juror, CTBUH

surface allows the space temperature to be higher than traditional all-air design solutions reducing energy consumption while maintaining occupant comfort.

Heating and cooling of the apartments is provided by vertical fan coil units. The horizontal sun screen blades provide shading on the east, south and west façades and reduce the energy consumption while minimizing the technical equipment requirements and maximizing occupant comfort.

Responsible uses of appropriate technologies provide an expressive means to realize this project in a sustainable way. The use of construction waste management techniques including diverting 50 to 75% of construction waste from landfills, the use of materials locally or regionally produced and manufactured, recycled materials and wood certified products, result in a significant reduction in environmental impact. Storm water filtration systems controlled flow drainage, use of storm water for irrigation and grey water systems all contribute to water conservation and the reduction in the use of potable municipal water resulting in saved utility charges and reduced impact on natural resources.

Jury Statement

Veer Towers takes on the responsibility of building an all glass tower in the desert environment of Las Vegas through its exquisitely detailed façades. The highly practicable solution of protecting the façades with a series of horizontal louvers is executed in such a way that adds vibrancy and interest to the buildings, and when combined with the use of colored glass and the countering leaning of each tower, creates a playful and dynamic addition, well suited to a city like Las Vegas.

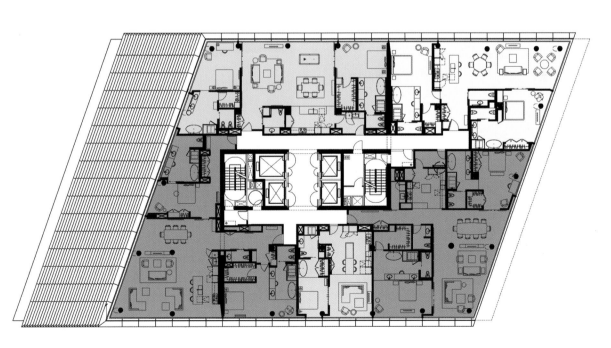

100 11th Avenue
New York, USA

A crystalline architectural beacon along the shore of the Hudson River, 100 11th Avenue utilizes a multi-pane panelized façade system to impart its signature shimmer to Manhattan's West Chelsea neighborhood. The main structure is clad with a panelized curtain wall system consisting of 1,650 windows, each a different size and uniquely oriented in space. Conceptually the tower is completely clad in clear glass, while outside views into the apartments are limited as light reflects off the randomly-oriented windows. Rather than reflecting one image, the façade reflects multiple images at the same time. Within the apartments, the floor-to-ceiling glass frames individual views as opposed to panoramic views. The shape of the building owes its uniqueness to curved long-span slabs that contour the corner of 19th Street and the Westside Highway.

The lower six stories of "podium" are encased by a double curtain wall system. The main building façade continues from the sixth floor down to the ground, while a second façade (the Street Wall) is offset 4.9m (16ft) towards the street. The atrium space created by these two faces is filled with an intricate mix of steel

Completion Date: June 2010
Height to Architectural Top[1]: 81m (265ft)
Stories[1]: 22
Area: 18,000 sq m (193,750 sq ft)
Primary Use[1]: Residential
Owner: Cape Advisors, Inc; Alf Naman Real Estate
Design Architect: Atelier Jean Nouvel
Associate Architect: Beyer Blinder Belle Architects
Structural Engineer: DeSimone Consulting Engineers
MEP Engineer: AKF Engineers
Main Contractor: Gotham Construction

Top: Overall view
Bottom: View of façade from interior
Opposite Left: Façade detail from exterior
Opposite Right: Typical floor plan

framing, concrete cantilevered walls, columns and balconies. This results in an indoor space in which trees are suspended overhead.

An elevated garden is located at the back of the building, supporting up to 2.4m (8ft) of soil and trees and incorporating a skylight opening. The space is structured with a 50.8cm (20in) thick slab spanning 10.7m (35ft) over a swimming pool below. To accommodate the unique façade weight and provide for the long clear spans, the typical 23cm (9in) slab thickens to double in depth at the curved edge of the building.

The building's lateral loads are resisted using a combination of core shear walls and elongated columns located throughout the building. In addition, studded structural steel was used at concrete link beams to accommodate large beam shear forces, and to limit beam depth. The main core is connected to two columns via in-slab outrigger beams at the curved edge to help minimize building deflections during earthquakes. The seven lateral columns dually provide support for the complex balcony structure that defines the lower stories.

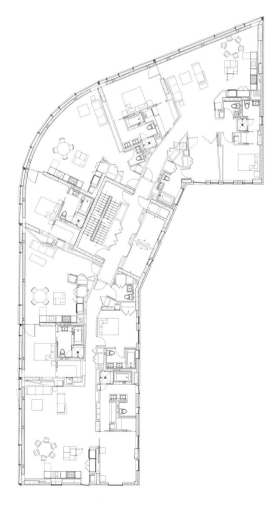

235 Van Buren

Chicago, USA

Located in the South Loop neighborhood of downtown Chicago, 235 Van Buren is a residential tower containing studios, and one- and two-bedroom condominiums targeted for people buying their first home. The site is located on the southern edge of the central business district of Chicago. Its architecture is a response to two site conditions. The first condition, to the north, is the densely in-filled context of the Chicago "Loop." The second condition, to the south, is an open space created by a freeway and traffic interchange which also contains a small park.

The articulation of the two masses is distinctly different to respond to these two conditions. The southern glass façade and random balconies provide a large-scale backdrop to the open space created by a major traffic interchange. A ribbon of concrete frames this glass wall, undulating to define the penthouse units and providing a large-scale gesture to the expressway as well as the taller buildings to the north. The random balconies express the individuality of the units within, providing a kinetic image from the freeway and helping shade the south facing glass.

Completion Date: March 2010
Height to Architectural Top[1]: 149m (490ft)
Stories[1]: 46
Area: 88,300 sq m (950,453 sq ft)
Primary Use[1]: Residential
Other Use: Retail
Owner/Developer: CMK Companies, Ltd
Design Architect: Perkins+Will
Structural Engineer: Tylk Gustafson Reckers Wilson Andrews, LLC
MEP Engineer: Cosentini Associates
Main Contractor: Bovis Lend Lease
Other Consultants: Terra Engineering, Ltd

Top: Overall view from the south
Bottom: Lobby entrance
Opposite Left: View from north east
Opposite Top Right: Ground floor plan
Opposite Bottom Right: Typical floor plan

The northern façade is a flush grid of rectangular openings with inset balconies. This gesture relates the building back to the historic Chicago Loop and the frame-expressed architecture of the "Chicago School."

In order to keep costs down and make the units more affordable, units are designed with borrowed-light bedrooms behind living spaces with 3m (10ft) ceilings to form a loft-like living arrangement. This allows the building to be wider than the standard residential tower and reduce exterior enclosure costs. In order to reduce the effect of this extra width, the overall mass of the building is broken down by dividing the tower into two slabs. This concept also provides an urban space at the street corner which relates to the existing plaza on the opposite corner and pronounces the entry to the residences. The massing break-down is further accentuated by differentiating the heights of the two shifted slabs at the top of the building. Principles of urban densification are incorporated into the design, with highly efficient unit planning and a district plant-sourced chilled-water supply. The building's green roof and capture of abundant natural light assist in cutting down overall energy costs.

300 East Randolph

Chicago, USA

3 00 East Randolph is a unique combination of a build-to-suit headquarters and a multi-tenant office tower in downtown Chicago. The design concept defined an initial building to serve a company's immediate needs and planned for vertical expansion in the future. Thus the building was constructed in two phases, with the second phase of construction occurring on top of the fully operational phase one, without interrupting existing tenant operations. The project's 33-story, first phase was completed in 1997 and in 2006 the decision was made to proceed with the initial plan and add 24 stories on top of the existing building. Nearly a decade separated the two phases of construction.

The initial foundations and structure were designed and constructed to support the fully expanded building. Additional riser space also was provided to accommodate independent mechanical, electrical and plumbing systems for the expansion floors. In order to allow the cooling towers on the roof of phase one to continue to serve the building during construction, a three-story gap from the 30th to the 33rd levels was left during construction. Once the new cooling

Completion Date: September 1997 (Phase 1); March 2010 (Phase 2)
Height to Architectural Top[1]: 227m (744ft)
Stories[1]: 54
Area: 217,756 sq m (2,343,906 sq ft)
Primary Use[1]: Office
Owner/Developer: Health Care Service Corporation
Design Architect: Goettsch Partners
Structural Engineer: C.S. Associates (Phase 1); Magnusson Klemencic Associates (Phase 2)
MEP Engineer: Cosentini Associates
Main Contractor: Walsh Construction
Other Consultants: One Lux Studio; Jenkins & Huntington; Cini-Little International; RKM Design Consultants

Top: Overall view from the south after Phase 2 completion, 2010
Bottom: Overall view from the south after Phase 1 completion, 1997
Opposite Left: Interior open stair
Opposite Right: Typical floor plans

towers were in place, 24 floors above the originals, the old cooling towers were removed, and cladding was applied. This space now serves as a mid-building conference center, providing necessary additional meeting and training space.

Vertical shafts to accommodate the high-zone elevators that service phase two of the project were accommodated in phase one as large atrium spaces that ran the height of the building alongside the low-zone elevator banks along the north wall. Local open stair cases are also located along the northern wall to promote inter-floor interactions without dependency on the elevators.

The entire exterior of the building is clad in glass, stainless steel and stone—all materials that both aged well and were easily matched as the building expanded. As a result of this design planning, there is no visible distinction between the old and new portions of the building, providing a seamless, integrated expression that now achieves its full height and appropriately fits into the Chicago skyline.

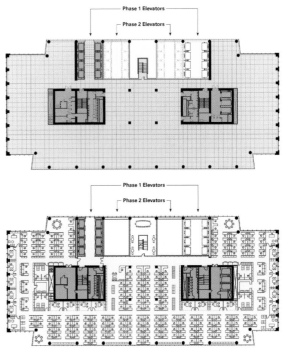

785 Eighth Avenue
New York, USA

The building sits on a particularly narrow site. Because of its 15:1 slenderness ratio (max ratio 18:1 on its east end), this building is one of the most slender structures in the world. The building was designed with due consideration given to its dynamic behavior. Designing an effective lateral system was a challenge, achieved by judicious placement of shear walls and the maximum possible utilization of slab-frame action. High strength concrete was used to increase stiffness.

The innovative concrete structure was clad in a butt-glazed curtain wall system in order to maximize the usable square footage inside an already slender floor plate, creating apartments that have frontage on more than one façade. A skillful use of architectural elements like the curtain wall coupled with structural cantilevers allows increased floor area at the top of the building. A row of cascading glass balconies on the east and west façades culminate in an iconic rooftop bulkhead transforming the building into a "glass artifact."

Top: Overall view looking up
Bottom: Typical unit interior

Completion Date: August 2009
Height to Architectural Top[1]: 157m (517ft)
Stories[1]: 42
Area: 11,612 sq m (125,000 sq ft)
Primary Use[1]: Residential
Other Use: Retail
Owner/Developer: 785 Partners, LLC; Esplanade Capital
Design Architect: Ismael Leyva Architects, PC
Structural Engineer: Ysrael A. Seinuk, PC
MEP Engineer: Ettinger Engineering Consultants
Main Contractor: Times Square Construction, Inc
Other Consultants: CPP Wind Engineering Consultants; Langan Engineering & Environmental Services

1450 Brickell
Miami, USA

Employing a very three dimensional, sculptural solution to its shape, the building's southern and eastern faces meet at a 75 degree angle; these two faces also inflect inward as they rise at approximately a two degree angle. In addition, irregular shapes which add to the building's thrust towards the corner project out 1m (3ft). The overall effect is that of a prism, where the glass takes on characteristics of a solid element. This continues up the building, which reaches a pinnacle at the south east corner.

Constructed in an active hurricane region, the all-glass façade is capable of withstanding 67+mps (150+mph) winds. As such, it offers the best protection against hurricanes of any building in Miami. Achieving this required thicker glass (which was already laminated to begin with), stronger connections and extrusions, and more steel in the wind pressure "hot spots." The glazing was tested repeatedly with a three-story mockup of the curtain wall. With the emergency generator backup system, the building has been designed to come through all but the very strongest storm undamaged, and being able to remain open for business immediately thereafter.

Top: Overall view from south east
Bottom: Façade detail at corner

Completion Date: January 2010
Height to Architectural Top[1]: 152m (500ft)
Stories[1]: 34
Area: 54,145 sq m (582,817 sq ft)
Primary Use[1]: Office
Owner: Park Place Holdings at Brickell LLC
Developer: Rilea Group
Design Architect: Nichols, Brosch, Wurst, Wolfe & Associates Inc
Structural Engineer: DeSimone Consulting Engineers
MEP Engineer: Steven Feller PE
Main Contractor: Coastal Construction
Other Consultants: CDC; RTKL Associates; PBS&J; Kimley-Horn

Banco Real Santander Headquarters
São Paulo, Brazil

The building was originally designed by a separate architect as the headquarters for the State Energy Company Eletropaulo, but was abandoned after the concrete structure was completed. The structure was known for more than ten years as "the skeleton," marring one of the most visible sites in São Paulo. In 2007 the challenging work of transforming an existing building shell into a completed design began. The result comprised of a glass tower with a single recess on each façade, creating the illusion of four slender glass buildings.

A sustainable approach was a key driver to the new design. With much of the building structure inherited, this approach focused on the use of local materials, energy efficiency, and the construction process. Rainwater and HVAC condensation is re-used for the landscape irrigation system and the high efficiency vacuum toilet system. All parking is located underground allowing almost 60% of the site area to be composed of vegetated open space. Further, the neighboring property is a public park, which was donated to the city by the construction company.

Completion Date: July 2009
Height to Architectural Top[1]: 135m (443ft)
Stories[1]: 28
Area: 85,000 sq m (914,932 sq ft)
Primary Use[1]: Office
Owner/Developer: WTorre Empreendimentos Imobiliários S.A.
Design Architect: Arquitectonica
Associate Architect: Washington Fiuza
Structural Engineer: Feitosa e Cruz
MEP Engineer: THERMOPLAN Engenharia Térmica Ltda; MHA Engenharia Ltda; TEMON Técnica de Montagens e Construções Ltda
Main Contractor: WTorre Engenharia

Top: Overall view at dusk
Bottom: Main lobby interior

Top: Overall view as seen from
street level

Cassa

New York, USA

Capitalizing on the site constraint of a narrow foot print, the slender obelisk-like profile demarcates its existence boldly. It furthers its uniqueness by cladding clean white metal against the conventional stone of its neighbors. The new building is flanked by two existing mid-rise buildings. Air rights over an adjoining building permitted the tower to reach its full height. Zoning restrictions for the area attempt to maximize the amount of sunlight on the pedestrian level by requiring deeper and deeper setbacks as buildings increase in height. These regulations have been interpreted in a contemporary way in Cassa by introducing an inclined plane with a slope of 88 degrees on the north wall. The structural system consists of a flat plate and reinforced concrete columns with those on West 45th Street sloped to follow the zoning sky exposure plane.

The primary source of cooling in all hotel suites and condominium residences is water-source heat pumps. Separate HVAC units air condition amenity spaces. Prefabricated metal panels with integrated fixed and operable windows provide a fully insulated wall system built in sections spanning floor-to-floor.

Completion Date: July 2010
Height to Architectural Top[1]: 146m (478ft)
Stories[1]: 45
Area: 15,815 sq m (170,231 sq ft)
Primary Use[1]: Mixed: Residential/Hotel
Owner: Solly Assa
Developer: Waterscape LLC
Design Architect: TEN Arquitectos; CetraRuddy
Structural Engineer: DeSimone Consulting Engineers
MEP Engineer: MG Engineering
Main Contractor: Pavarini McGovern
Other Consultants: Front; Jenkins & Huntington; SMW

The Clare at Water Tower
Chicago, USA

Unique in its program, this project houses a Continuing Care Retirement Community as well as new education space for Loyola University. The project is unusual in that the functional elements, usually distributed in several buildings in a typical CCRC, have been stacked vertically. The program consists of a tower with 271 independent living units, 39 assisted living units, 45 skilled nursing units and a base of parking, retail and Loyola classrooms. Located on the roof of the tower podium is a "healing" garden.

Despite its mixed program, it was a design imperative that the building not become a mix of varying floor-to-floor heights with multiple fenestration patterns, but rather a cohesive high-rise tower with base, shaft, and top. This was accomplished by a strong, single tower design reading from ground to level 53 and a subservient podium massing. The tower has a very rigorous, repetitive fenestration pattern that was designed to align with all of the varying functional plans. The ABA window module accommodates the various partition layouts of the different uses.

Completion Date: March 2009
Height to Architectural Top[1]: 179m (589ft)
Stories[1]: 53
Area: 69,677 sq m (749,997 sq ft)
Primary Use[1]: Residential
Other Use: Educational
Owner: Franciscan Sisters of Chicago Service Corporation
Developer: Greystone Communities
Design Architect: Perkins+Will
Structural Engineer: Thornton Tomasetti
MEP Engineer: WMA Consulting Engineers
Main Contractor: Bovis/McHugh JV
Other Consultants: Hoerr Schaudt Landscape Architecture; AECOM/STS

Top: Overall night view from north
Bottom: View of podium and garden

Fairmont Pacific Rim

Vancouver, Canada

The mixed-used characteristics of the building are reflected in the bold architectural expression of the east and south façades, articulated by the subtle treatment of balconies and slab edges and further differentiated by the integration of a public art installation on the lower hotel. Vancouver's Public Art Program requires every project that is re-zoned over 9,300 sq m (100,000 sq ft) to contribute to a public art process approved by the City. This is the first time that artwork has been integrated onto the building façades and can be interpreted as part of the elevation.

The public artwork by British artist Liam Gillick wraps around the south and east faces in a repeated line of running text with no spacing between words or punctuation: *Lyingontopofthebuilding… Lyingontopofthebuilding…Lyingontopofthebuilding… thecloudslooknonearerthanwheniwaslyingonthestreet* The 61cm (2ft) stainless steel letters were strategically placed to interplay with the architectural expression and its materiality reflects the ambient lighting condition and surrounding color. Such "codependence" between art and architecture is a bold and unique attempt at this scale.

Top: Overall view from the south west
Bottom: Façade detail with art installation

Completion Date: April 2010
Height to Architectural Top[1]: 140m (460ft)
Stories[1]: 46
Area: 75,997 sq m (818,025 sq ft)
Primary Use[1]: Mixed: Residential/Hotel
Owner/Developer: Westbank Project Corp.; Peterson Investment Group Inc
Design Architect: James K.M. Cheng Architects Inc
Structural Engineer: Jones Kwong Kishi Consulting
MEP Engineer: Sterling, Cooper & Associates
Main Contractor: 299 Burrard Landing
Other Consultants: Phillips Farevaag Smallenberg; Nemetz (S/A) & Associates Ltd

Freeport-McMoRan Center

Phoenix, USA

Freeport-McMoRan Center is part of a recent rebirth within downtown Phoenix and incorporates current office and environmental strategies. The building design is a critical response to the existing context of seemingly opaque high-rise office buildings designed to protect occupants from the desert sun's intense heat gain and glare. The building takes the opposite approach by using transparency and incorporating current glass technology and a high-performance curtain wall system, along with innovative shading to provide sun control. Programmatically the building is unique to the Phoenix market by taking a large office plate typically found in suburban office buildings and placing it on top of a stacked parking structure.

The building is sited north of Phoenix's existing high-rise core surrounded by the new development of the Arizona State University Downtown Campus and Civic Park. The building is also located across the street from the central bus transit hub and new light rail station making it one of the newest large-scale transit oriented development projects in Phoenix.

Completion Date: November 2009
Height to Architectural Top[1]: 104m (342ft)
Stories[1]: 26
Area: 75,746 sq m (815,323 sq ft)
Primary Use[1]: Office
Owner: Central Park East Associates, LLC
Developer: Mesirow Financial
Design Architect: SmithGroup
Structural Engineer: Paul Koehler Consulting Structural Engineers
MEP Engineer: SmithGroup
Main Contractor: Holder Construction
Other Consultants: Evans Kuhn & Associates Inc; Laskin & Associates

Top: Overall view from south west
Bottom: East façade detail
Opposite Left: South façade detail with dichroic glass feature
Opposite Right: East–west (top) and south (bottom) façade strategy diagrams

The transparency of the building is allowed by appropriate building orientation and varying shading strategies. On the south façade two 61cm (2ft) deep horizontal sun shades per floor provide shading while doubling as a light shelf bringing natural light deep into each floor plate. The east and west façades use a 61cm (2ft) vertical sunshade blocking out low angle sun. Additionally, to supplement the performance of the east and west façade a ceramic frit with a 15% coverage in a gradient pattern increases the shading coefficient of the glass.

Large efficient floor plates with floor-to-ceiling glass characterize the office program. The building corners were expressed by eliminating the corner columns and cantilevering the plate 4.6m (15ft). This gives the corners of the building a visual significance while offering unobstructed views from the interior. The integrated parking structure is naturally ventilated. By using perforated standing seam metal panels the design was able to accommodate views, airflow and natural light.

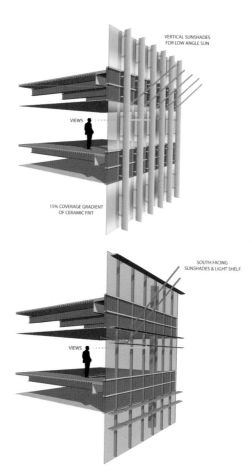

LA Live Hotel and Residences
Los Angeles, USA

LA Live is the first high-rise to be built in Downtown Los Angeles in 20 years, making it the first building to have a significant impact on the skyline in the same period. LA Live and its distinctive tower fill a long-standing void in the southwest corner of the downtown area as bounded by the cornerstones of the Disney Concert Hall, Los Angeles City Hall and the financial, garment and jewelry districts.

The building expands horizontally as it rises vertically, reflecting the varied programs within. Each succeeding use—22 JW Marriott Los Angeles at LA Live floors at the bottom, followed by four floors of The Ritz-Carlton Hotel Los Angeles, and the Ritz-Carlton Residences at the top—has larger space requirements. The building's elegantly curving curtain wall smoothes the jagged transition among the changing floor plates as they stack skyward.

The three-story lobby is a pass-through space that provides access from Olympic Boulevard to the Nokia Theatre and Nokia Plaza. The lobby is the urban connection between Downtown and LA Live, the

Completion Date: March 2010
Height to Architectural Top[1]: 203m (667ft)
Stories[1]: 54
Area: 149,597 sq m (1,610,247 sq ft)
Primary Use[1]: Mixed: Residential/Hotel
Other Use: Convention Center
Owner/Developer: AEG
Design Architect: Gensler
Structural Engineer: Nabih Youssef Associates
MEP Engineer: ACCO; SASCO; Murray Company; Western States
Main Contractor: Webcor
Other Consultants: Herrick Steel

Top: Overall view from the north east
Bottom: Construction view of steel shear wall
Opposite Top Left: Typical floor plan
Opposite Bottom Right: Typical section

Staples Center and Los Angeles Convention Center. The building features two outdoor decks with pools, bars and events facilities.

The tower takes full advantage of a new leading edge Performance Based structural steel lateral force resisting system, comprised of un-stiffened thin steel plate shear walls (SPSW). It is the first high-rise to use this technology in California. Using 6.4-9.5mm (0.25-0.375in) thick steel plate shear walls as opposed to 76cm (30in) thick concrete columns created increased usable square footage, and creating a lighter building

allowed the addition of four floors to the tower while creating better views on every floor without the necessary moment frames common in steel design. Switching to Steel Plate Shear Walls also saved millions of dollars in construction costs and shaved four months off the production schedule. The hotel tower also consists of steel moment frames, Buckling Restrained Braces (BRB), mid-height outriggers and cap trusses. The design process exemplifies a successful collaboration of performance-based engineering and rigorous peer review by a panel of noted experts in each structural system type.

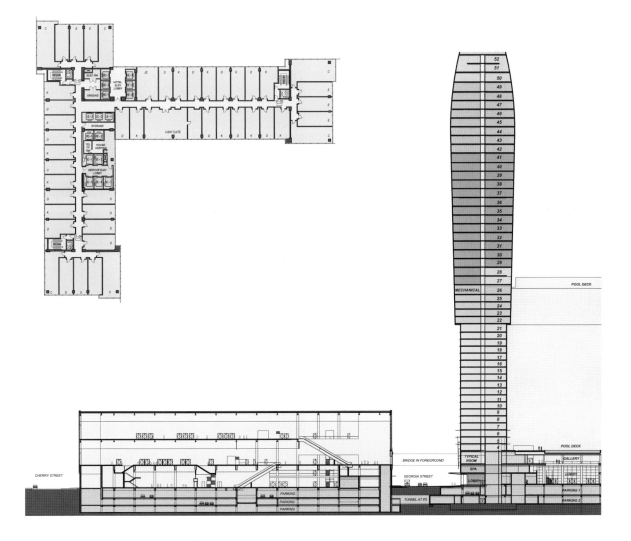

The Legacy

Chicago, USA

The Legacy at Millennium Park is a residential tower that rises from the heart of Chicago's Loop while seamlessly interacting at street level with the fabric of its landmark neighborhood. The tower maximizes its urban site, incorporating 356 residences and associated amenities with academic space for the School of the Art Institute of Chicago (SAIC), expanded athletic facilities for the century-old University Club, retail, and residential parking.

The building site is within the Jeweler's Row Historic District, surrounded by landmark buildings. The development restored the façades of three vacant six-story buildings on the site, and incorporates them into the base of the tower. The Legacy lobby is within the SAIC building and the parking entrance is through the façades on Wabash. The project effectively and thoroughly integrates itself into its existing ground plane context. Building setbacks above the façades allow the Legacy to fit with its small-scaled neighbors. A portion of the tower cantilevers over a private alley on the east side to accent the slender profile of the building from the park and augment the lakefront views to the north and south.

Completion Date: April 2010
Height to Architectural Top[1]: 249m (818ft)
Stories[1]: 73
Area: 99,649 sq m (1,072,612 sq ft)
Primary Use[1]: Residential
Developer: Monroe/Wabash Development LLC
Design Architect: Solomon Cordwell Buenz
Associate Architect: McGuire Igleski (historic preservation)
Structural Engineer: C.S. Associates
MEP Engineer: WMA Consulting Engineers
Main Contractor: Walsh Construction

Top: Overall view from the north east
Bottom: Restored Wabash Avenue façades (on left)

Top: Overall night view
Bottom: Interior sky lobby

Mandarin Oriental

Las Vegas, USA

The new Mandarin Oriental Las Vegas contains a 400-room hotel and 215-unit branded condominium tower on top of a multi-use base with ballroom and retail functions. The project is prominently sited on Las Vegas Boulevard situated within the new CityCenter mixed-use development. This unique context affords the project two distinct opportunities: on a macro level, the building acts as a gateway into Las Vegas; on the micro level, the building conveys a sense of seclusion for hotel guests, creating a city within a city.

The façade is a layered interlocking motif of vertical aluminum panels and high-performance, low-E glass with ceramic horizontal frit. From the interior, the frit provides various levels of transparency, allowing for open, naturally illuminated spaces in public areas and shaded, screened areas where more privacy is desired. To reduce solar heat gain and to conserve energy, heavily insulated spandrel panels are used to increase the percentage of opaque cladding area. The façade system accounts for about 9% of the building's total energy savings.

Completion Date: December 2009
Height to Architectural Top[1]: 164m (539ft)
Stories[1]: 47
Area: 92,900 sq m (999,967 sq ft)
Primary Use[1]: Mixed: Residential/Hotel
Owner: Mandarin Oriental
Developer: MGM Mirage Design Group; Infinity World Development Corporation
Design Architect: Kohn Pedersen Fox Associates
Associate Architect: Adamson Associates
Structural Engineer: Halcrow Yolles
MEP Engineer: WSP Flack + Kurtz
Main Contractor: Perini Building Company
Other Consultants: Adam Tihany Associates

RBC Centre
Toronto, Canada

RBC and RBC Dexia, the primary tenants of the building, required a design that supported their corporate objectives of economic, social and environmental sustainability. Working together with the developer, a vision of a superior workplace to dramatically improve occupant comfort, space planning flexibility, and higher environmental sustainability standards was developed within the market driven framework of capital and operating cost responsibility.

This project showcases the owner/developer Cadillac Fairview's GREEN AT WORK™ initiative which is a detailed, measurable and long-term program which is national in scope; implemented at all properties and sets operational benchmarks to reduce energy consumption and waste, improve environmental protection, and encourages sustainable procurement. Strategies implemented at RBC Centre include: a green roof amenity, flexible raised access flooring, computer-controlled solar shading and daylight harvesting, sun-sensor and occupancy-sensor controlled lighting, rain water reuse for toilet flushing and stormwater management, and operable windows on the podium.

Top: Overall view from the north
Bottom: Street view of tower podium

Completion Date: June 2009
Height to Architectural Top[1]: 185m (607ft)
Stories[1]: 42
Area: 127,300 sq m (1,370,246 sq ft)
Primary Use[1]: Office
Owner/Developer: The Cadillac Fairview Corporation Limited
Design Architect: Kohn Pedersen Fox Associates; Sweeny Sterling Finlayson & Co Architects Inc
Associate Architect: B+H Architects
Structural Engineer: Halcrow Yolles
MEP Engineer: The Mitchell Partnership; Mulvey & Banani Intl.
Main Contractor: PCL Constructors
Other Consultants: Strybos Barron King Ltd; Schaeffers Consulting Engineers; Enermodal Engineering Ltd

Top: Overall view from north east
Bottom: Building entry

Sackville-Dundas Residences
Toronto, Canada

This project inaugurated the first phase of the redevelopment of Regent Park—Canada's largest and oldest public housing project. It addresses the main objectives of area revitalization—mixed housing and income, safety, and sustainable design—while also contributing to resident quality of life and the area's architectural fabric.

The project consists of two buildings, resting on a low podium facing a future neighborhood park to the east. The southern low-rise building contains 75 family units, while the northern high-rise tower contains 150 seniors' units. Beneath the building are two levels of underground parking as well as the district heating and cooling cogeneration plant that will service the entire Regent Park community. An increased level of amenity was created through the raised garden court, roof gardens, landscaped outdoor spaces, retail and community spaces. Key design strategies include natural day lighting for all occupied spaces, reduced energy consumption through the Community Energy System, conservation of potable water, and passive solar shading throughout the building design.

Completion Date: May 2009
Height to Architectural Top[1]: 84m (274ft)
Stories[1]: 22
Area: 11,585 sq m (124,700 sq ft)
Primary Use[1]: Residential
Owner/Developer: Toronto Community Housing Corporation
Design Architect: architectsAlliance
Associate Architect: Graziani + Corazza Architects Inc
Structural Engineer: Sigmund Soudack & Associates Inc
MEP Engineer: LKM Consulting Engineers
Main Contractor: Daniels Corporation

Shangri-la

Vancouver, Canada

Shangri-la is the first building in the City of Vancouver to be approved for additional height over the city maximum of 137m (450ft). The site is located in a transitional area between the central business district and a predominantly residential area to the west. Although a mixed-use building reflects this transition, the tower design de-emphasizes the different uses to present a unified, restrained language. The site is significant, being one of only two downtown properties where a tower development could be located outside all restrictive city view cones, and thus qualify for the maximum discretionary height increase. These view cones preserve views of the local North Shore Mountains from various strategic vantage points around Vancouver. The view cone boundary cuts diagonally across the eastern side of the lot, restricting the tower to the eastern corner. Respecting that diagonal view cone line was the main influence on the tower's wedge-shaped form.

Of the 121m (396ft) long site, only the eastern most 30m (100ft) could be developed to full height. This allowed for an extensive podium and plaza complex to be constructed. To animate the street front around

Completion Date: April 2009
Height to Architectural Top[1]: 201m (659ft)
Stories[1]: 59
Area: 61,300 sq m (659,828 sq ft)
Primary Use[1]: Mixed: Residential/Hotel
Owner/Developer: KBK #11 Ventures Ltd
Design Architect: James K.M. Cheng Architects Inc
Structural Engineer: Jones Kwong Kishi Consulting
MEP Engineer: Sterling, Cooper & Associates
Main Contractor: Ledcor Construction Ltd
Other Consultants: Phillips Farevaag Smallenberg; Nemetz (S/A) & Associates Ltd

Top: Overall view from the west
Bottom: Roof garden
Opposite Left: Aerial view of podium
Opposite Right: Roof plan with residential amenities

the tower, substantial amenity space has been built facing outward toward the street to engage the pedestrian. The space includes a spa, retail tenancies, and a public art site. A "bamboo grove" was planted along an outdoor stair which leads to additional upper level restaurant space. Green roofs are planted on the podium roofs as well as two private roof gardens for use by the residents of the tower.

The corner façades present a formal appearance of floating glass planes, animated by a pattern of square luminescent panels off-set from the glass skin. They are a composite comprised of a luminescent coating, chromatic film and textured glass that absorb energy from daylight and surrounding light sources and then glow from that energy in the evening. They change color when viewed from different vantage points and under different weather conditions. These luminescent grids are intended as veils, held off the glass surface on the corner façades and in practical terms, they conceal the building exhaust vents in the curtain wall skin behind. They required no wiring and consume no energy.

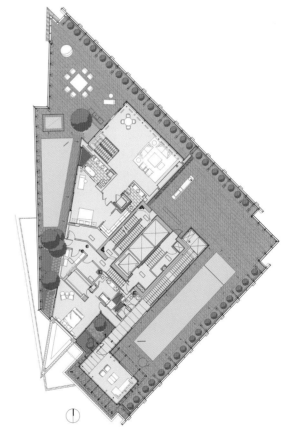

The Standard, New York

New York, USA

The building straddles the High Line, an abandoned section of a 75-year-old elevated railroad line, which passes over the buildings of the district and is currently being developed as a new linear public park. Muscular, sculptural piers, which clearly remove the building from the orthogonal street grid, raise the building 17.4m (57ft), allowing the horizontally-scaled industrial landscape to pass beneath it and natural light to penetrate to the street. To accommodate the client's desire that this structure reflect the character of the neighborhood, reclaimed brick, steel frame windows and a metal canopy similar to the existing Meatpacking plants and other warehouses were utilized at the lower levels.

The eastern half of the structure is supported by a single 1.5m thick x 15.2m wide x 18.3m tall (5ft x 50ft x 60ft) sloping concrete wall—the East Pier. To span the Highline at the eastern half of the site, a transfer system comprised of two 65 ksi steel trusses was utilized. The top chords of the trusses are embedded in a 0.9m (3ft) deep concrete transfer slab, creating a large double-tee beam.

Completion Date: September 2009
Height to Architectural Top[1]: 80m (261ft)
Stories[1]: 19
Area: 18,580 sq m (200,000 sq ft)
Primary Use[1]: Hotel
Owner: Andre Balazs Properties
Developer: The John Buck Company
Design Architect: Ennead Architects (formerly Polshek Partnership Architects)
Structural Engineer: DeSimone Consulting Engineers
MEP Engineer: Edwards & Zuck Engineers
Main Contractor: Pavarini McGovern
Other Consultants: Langan Engineering & Environmental Services; H.A. Bader; Cerami & Associates; Shawn Hausman, Roman & Williams

Top: Overall view with High Line passing underneath
Bottom: Construction view of steel truss spanning the High Line

Top: Overall night view from south west
Bottom: Street view of south west corner building entrance

theWit Hotel
Chicago, USA

The building is an active participant in its neighborhood with its signature chartreuse "lightning bolt," a contemporary expression of differentiation addressing the corner condition of the site. Located at the northern gateway of the newly revitalized State Street Theater and retail corridor, and steps away from Millennium Park, the zigzagging glass was designed as a "marquee" for the building, contributing to the theatricality of the district. The project has transformed a diminutive 883 sq m (9,500 sq ft) parcel of land in a key downtown corridor, which had languished over the past 30 years, into a vibrant building that includes 298 hotel rooms; a 40 seat state-of-the-art multimedia digital theater; three restaurants; a full-service spa; and banquet and meeting space.

In an effort to set a new standard in the hospitality technology arena, theWit employs groundbreaking technology for in-room guest entertainment and guest communication, providing greater efficiency and responsiveness, incorporating interactive lobby & meeting room displays, Networked IP mini bars, and Networked IP HVAC controls.

Completion Date: May 2009
Height to Architectural Top[1]: 95m (311ft)
Stories[1]: 26
Area: 22,498 sq m (242,166 sq ft)
Primary Use[1]: Hotel
Owner/Developer: ECD Company
Design Architect: Koo and Associates Ltd
Structural Engineer: Halvorson and Partners
MEP Engineer: Design/Build
Main Contractor: McHugh Construction

Titanium La Portada

Santiago, Chile

The building's design was inspired by the very essence of the "La Portada" area, a geographical gateway shaped by wind and the ice water river flow from the Andes since the ancient glacial period. The main tower's two glass façades simulate soaring wind-filled sails plying the urban torrent. The visual energy generated by this arrangement is further enhanced by numerous urban features converging to the site, transforming the building into a physical and symbolic referent at the metropolitan level. Also, the building transmits its dynamic energy through vertical cuts in the curved façades along with the helical arrangement of the decks.

The façade reflects the heartbeat of a living, constantly changing environment nourished by the city's main arteries. The crowning oval rooftop seems to levitate above the building's ethereal glass sails—a metaphor for the physical challenges involved, met and overcome to realize this project for Chile's capital. The Titanium name comes from the metal alloy; a resistant, durable and viable long-lasting element.

Completion Date: February 2010
Height to Architectural Top[1]: 195m (640ft)
Stories[1]: 55
Area: 132,736 sq m (1,428,758 sq ft)
Primary Use[1]: Office
Owner/Developer: Inmobiliaria Titanium S.A.
Design Architect: Abraham Senerman Lamas
Structural Engineer: Alfonso Larraín
MEP Engineer: Masterclima
Main Contractor: Constructora SENARCO
Other Consultants: SIRVE; Miranda&Nasi

Top: Overall view
Bottom: Building lobby interior
Opposite Left: Façade detail with balconies
Opposite Right: Typical floor plan

The building's erection was only possible due to the development of an anti-seismic technology, contained in several energy dissipaters distributed up along the height of the building. Shortly before the building's official opening this system was put to the test when a magnitude 8.8 earthquake struck Chile in February 2010. The building survived this monumental seismic event unscathed. The building's facade is also seismic resistant, with its insulated laminated glass used throughout the entire building. Additional safety features include fireproof pressurized elevators for emergency operation, two pressurized staircases, two external ladders for emergency evacuation and a double helipad on the roof.

The tower has set a new environmental standard for high-rise architecture in Chile, implementing strategies such as: energy behavior monitoring, natural ventilation through operable awning windows, recycling stations on every floor, high-efficiency thermo-panel walls which maximize the entrance of light while filtering solar radiation. Further, more than 70% of the ground level is dedicated to gardens, passages, squares and galleries for the public.

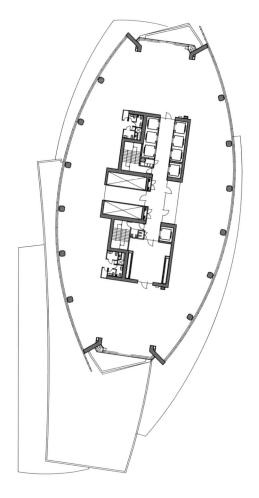

Toren

New York, USA

Combining a playful variety of insulated glass units and metal panels, the curtain wall creates a shimmering mix of opacity and transparency. Rather than employing a typical repetitive expression, the Toren enclosure is articulated as a binary opposition between vertical and horizontal lines which move rhythmically up the building. The panels feature embossed circles, representing the round blossoms of the Myrtle tree, the name of the primary street on which the building is sited. In all, the Toren's exterior skin uses 200 unique panels in size and shape creating a seemingly random arrangement in which there is not one floor identical to another.

Toren features an on-site cogeneration plant in which five 100 kiloWATT generators fuel the building's electrical, heating and cooling. The units use natural gas-fired reciprocating engines in a computer controlled package to make electricity. Hot water heat is then recovered from the engines and combustion exhaust and used for building heat, domestic hot water and absorber air conditioning. Should the local grid ever fail, the cogeneration system will be able to provide emergency power for the building.

Above: Overall view from the north west

Completion Date: April 2010
Height to Architectural Top[1]: 130m (427ft)
Stories[1]: 37
Area: 23,433 sq m (252,231 sq ft)
Primary Use[1]: Residential
Owner/Developer: BFC Partners
Design Architect: Skidmore, Owings & Merrill LLP
Structural Engineer: Severud Associates Consulting Engineers
MEP Engineer: Integrated Energy Concepts
Main Contractor: BFC Construction
Other Consultants: Israel Berger & Associates; Van Deusen & Associates; Cerami & Associates

Torre Libertad
Mexico City, Mexico

Torre Libertad is on the Paseo de la Reforma, Mexico City's grand historic boulevard. Near Chapultapec Park on a stretch of the thoroughfare recently reinvigorated by new development, the building overlooks a prominent roundabout featuring the landmark Diana Fountain. In response to this historic site, the design of the tower is simple and sculptural. The tower is a curved, triangular form with a carefully proportioned curtain wall of clear glass and white aluminum sunshades. The corner facing the Diana Fountain features an undulating facet that catches the changing light while framing a view of the fountain. This facet tapers as it reaches toward the sky and curves outward as it approaches the ground, creating a canopy over the entry.

The tower houses the St. Regis Hotel, with 189 guest rooms, and the St. Regis Residences, with 100 apartments. The tower's plan and structural system allow for generous layouts for each unit. Residents and visitors enter the ground-floor entrance into a lobby atrium. The hotel reception is on the fourth level, which opens onto a wide landscaped terrace.

Completion Date: October 2009
Height to Architectural Top[1]: 150m (492ft)
Stories[1]: 31
Area: 77,500 sq m (834 203 sq ft)
Primary Use[1]: Mixed: Residential/Hotel
Owner/Developer: Grupo Ideurban
Design Architect: Pelli Clarke Pelli Architects
Associate Architect: Grupo Ideurban
Structural Engineer: Enrique Martinex Romero
MEP Engineer: CYVSA
Main Contractor: Grupo Ideurban

Top: Overall view with Diana Fountain and roundabout in foreground
Bottom: View down lobby atrium

Vdara Hotel & Spa

Las Vegas, USA

Part of the new CityCenter development, Vdara is distinguished by its slender profile and curvature, which respond to Harmon Circle and the interlocking arcs of the ARIA Resort & Casino located across the shared circular drive. Rising to varying heights, the two outer bars fall away to reveal a slender center bar rising above, while these shifted arcs give the impression of three discrete building volumes slipping one against another. This effect is reinforced by the slightly recessed circulation corridors between them. Alternating bands of reflective vision glass and light-diffusing, acid-etched spandrel glass in black and white are set off on different planes to achieve a unique shimmering texture on the façade.

In order to increase the view frontage along the curtain wall, the 1,495 rooms are wider than those of most hotel buildings. The floor plan is devoted almost entirely to apartment space, with a double-loaded corridor passing through the interstitial spaces separating the arcs. This results in a highly efficient circulation strategy. The main elevator core passes through the center of the building, where the arcs overlap and there is no perimeter exposure, reducing wasted space.

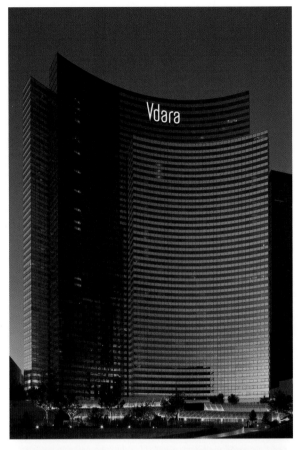

Top: Overall night view
Bottom: Building entry

Completion Date: December 2009
Height to Architectural Top[1]: 169m (556ft)
Stories[1]: 66
Area: 128,900 sq m (1,387,468 sq ft)
Primary Use[1]: Hotel
Owner/Developer: MGM Mirage Design Group
Design Architect: RV Architecture, LLC
Associate Architect: Leo A. Daly
Structural Engineer: DeSimone Consulting Engineers; Lockwood, Andrews & Newnam, Inc
MEP Engineer: Cosentini Associates
Main Contractor: Perini Building Company
Other Consultants: Lochsa Engineering LLC; Curtain Wall Design & Consulting, Inc; BBG-BBGM

Ventura Corporate Towers

Rio de Janeiro, Brazil

Ventura Corporate Towers was constructed in two phases, beginning in April of 2006 with the east tower. Excavation work for the west tower did not commence until after the east tower had already reached structural topping out. The towers are a mirrored reflection of one another directly abutting from their basement levels to the 24th floor before stepping back for their remaining height, which extends to the maximum allowable by current zoning laws for the city. Like the two towers, a connected parking structure on the north side of the buildings was also constructed in two parts directly abutting and mirroring one another.

The towers are nearly square in form with a triangular bevel in the south façade that starts wide and narrows as it goes up the height of the tower—making a direct reference to the neighboring Metropolitan Cathedral which is conical in form. Green plated glass elements form prisms and surfaces in contrast to the continuous rigid granite east and west faces which wrap up the building forming an "L" over the roofs, further unifying the two towers as one architectural expression.

Top: Overall view from south east
Bottom: Aerial context view from the north showing phase two under construction

Completion Date: June 2010
Height to Architectural Top[1]**:** 151m (497ft)
Stories[1]**:** 34
Area: 169,411 sq m (1,823,524 sq ft)
Primary Use[1]**:** Office
Owner/Developer: Tishman Speyer; BTS
Design Architect: Aflalo & Gasperini Architects; Kohn Pedersen Fox Associates
Structural Engineer: JKMF
MEP Engineer: MHA Engenharia Ltda
Main Contractor: Tishman Speyer; Camargo Corrêa Desenvolvimento Imobiliário

William Beaver House

New York, USA

Manipulation of form, colors, and materials were central to the project's design to achieve a distinctive presence on the skyline. This is achieved through the use of highly reflective glazed brick that modulates down the façade, gradually receding to shift pride of place to the public/semi-public building base. The base is a highly contextual anchor that is lifted and carved away to reveal and engage the street with the building's activities. At the base the sidewalks are widened, and a small piazza is created lending private property for much needed public space. The tower's perceived mass is reduced by "breaking" the corner, separating the two street façades.

The project deliberately conflates and blurs the realms of housing and hospitality, domesticity and public life, privacy and sociability. The residential program fills the tower above, which is set back from the base to form a housing core. That core is brought down to, and formally interlocks with, the more public, extroverted base. At once, the residential and public components are co-joined and revealed.

Completion Date: January 2010
Height to Architectural Top[1]: 161m (527ft)
Stories[1]: 47
Area: 37,084 sq m (399,176 sq ft)
Primary Use[1]: Residential
Owner/Developer: SDS Investments LLC;
Andre Balazs Properties
Design Architect: TsAO & McKOWN Architects
Associate Architect: SLCE Architects, LLP
Structural Engineer: DeSimone Consulting Engineers
MEP Engineer: I.M. Robbins Consulting Engineers
Main Contractor: Bovis Lend Lease
Other Consultants: M. Paul Friedberg and Partners

Top: Overall view from river
Bottom: Brick façade detail
Opposite Top Left: Ground floor plan
Opposite Bottom Left: Typical floor plan
Opposite Right: East elevation

The project engages the street with public activities (an indoor/outdoor restaurant) and semi-public activities such as a residents' lounge, and on the second floor various leisure and recreational uses that also open onto the street. The architectural forms are thus given greater meaning, and community is fostered between the building's residents and their neighbors.

To help build community among the building's residents, and simultaneously, to imbue greater meaning into the architectural resolution of the building's top, nearly half of the penthouse floor is given to common areas and terraces to be enjoyed by all residents. Within the compact apartments, space is maximized, in part, by joining sleeping and bathing areas.

Architectural form and material choice addressed issues of sustainability, rather than reliance on advanced systems. The opaque cladding area is more than 95% brick, composed of clay that was sourced and manufactured locally. Additionally, judicious choices in the balance between glazed areas and heavily insulated walls deliver energy conservation that exceeds New York City's code requirements.

1075 Peachtree
Atlanta, USA

Completion Date: April 2010
Height to Architectural Top[1]: North Tower: 149m (488ft); South Tower: 125m (410ft)
Stories[1]: North Tower: 38; South Tower: 39
Area: 139,354 sq m (1,500,000 sq ft)
Primary Use[1]: North Tower: Office; South Tower: Mixed: Residential/Hotel
Other Use: Retail
Owner: Daniel Corporation; Selig Enterprises
Developer: Daniel Corporation
Design Architect: Rule Joy Trammell + Rubio LLC
Structural Engineer: Stanley D. Lindsey & Associates Ltd
MEP Engineer: Jordan & Skala Engineers
Main Contractor: Brasfield & Gorrie

353 North Clark Street
Chicago, USA

Completion Date: November 2009
Height to Architectural Top[1]: 190m (623ft)
Stories[1]: 44
Area: 133,780 sq m (1,439,995 sq ft)
Primary Use[1]: Office
Owner: SPD LLC
Developer: Mesirow Financial
Design Architect: Lohan Anderson LLC
Associate Architect: Epstein
Structural Engineer: Epstein
MEP Engineer: Environmental Systems Design, Inc
Main Contractor: Bovis Lend Lease

510 Madison
New York, USA

Completion Date: September 2010
Height to Architectural Top[1]: 138m (452ft)
Stories[1]: 31
Area: 27,346 sq m (294,349 sq ft)
Primary Use[1]: Office
Owner/Developer: Macklowe Properties
Design Architect: MOED de ARMAS & SHANNON Architects; SLCE Architects, LLP
Structural Engineer: Gilsanz Murray Steficek LLP
MEP Engineer: I.M. Robbins Consulting Engineers
Main Contractor: Tishman Construction

[1] For all definitions used in the data sections throughout this book, refer to CTBUH criteria shown on pages 184–187

The Brooklyner
New York, USA

Completion Date: 2009
Height to Architectural Top[1]: 162m (531ft)
Stories[1]: 52
Area: 42,905 sq m (140,764 sq ft)
Primary Use[1]: Residential
Owner/Developer: The Clarett Group
Design Architect: GKV Architects
Structural Engineer: WSP Cantor Seinuk
MEP Engineer: Cosentini Associates
Main Contractor: Bovis Lend Lease

Cosmopolitan Resort & Casino
Las Vegas, USA

Completion Date: August 2010
Height to Architectural Top[1]: 184m (604ft)
Stories[1]: 52
Area: 604,000 sq m (6,500,000 sq ft)
Primary Use[1]: East Tower: Residential; West Tower: Hotel
Other Use: Casino
Owner: The Cosmopolitan of Las Vegas
Design Architect: Arquitectonica
Associate Architect: Friedmutter Group
Structural Engineer: DeSimone Consulting Engineers
MEP Engineer: FEA Consulting Engineers; RHR Consulting Engineers
Main Contractor: Perini Building Company
Other Consultants: Martin & Martin; The RJA Group, Inc

The Elysian
Chicago, USA

Completion Date: November 2009
Height to Architectural Top[1]: 214m (701ft)
Stories[1]: 60
Area: 53,846 sq m (579,600 sq ft)
Primary Use[1]: Mixed: Residential/Hotel
Other Use: Retail
Owner: First Elysian Properties LLC
Developer: The Elysian Development Group – Chicago LLC
Design Architect: Lucien Lagrange Architects LTD
Structural Engineer: Halvorson and Partners
MEP Engineer: Advanced Mechanical Systems, Inc; Gurtz Electric Company; Great Lakes
Main Contractor: McHugh Construction
Other Consultants: Daniel Weinbach and Associates

Met 2
Miami, USA

Completion Date: West Tower: May 2010; East Tower: September 2010
Height to Architectural Top[1]: West Tower: 199m (655ft); East Tower: 153m (502ft)
Stories[1]: West Tower: 47; East Tower: 41
Area: 212,525 sq m (2,287,600 sq ft)
Primary Use[1]: West Tower: Office; East Tower: Hotel
Owner/Developer: P & G Tract "C" Development Ltd
Design Architect: Nichols, Brosch, Wurst, Wolfe & Associates Inc
Structural Engineer: Ysrael A. Seinuk, PC
MEP Engineer: HNGS Engineers
Main Contractor: Suffolk Construction Company Inc
Other Consultants: VSN Engineers; RTKL Associates; Kimley-Horn

Residences at the Ritz-Carlton
Philadelphia, USA

Completion Date: July 2009
Height to Architectural Top[1]: 158m (518ft)
Stories[1]: 46
Area: 57,383 sq m (617,665 sq ft)
Primary Use[1]: Residential
Owner/Developer: AGC Partners, LP
Design Architect: Handel Architects LLP
Structural Engineer: Thornton Tomasetti
MEP Engineer: WSP Flack + Kurtz
Main Contractor: L.F. Driscoll Co
Other Consultants: Pennoni Associates Inc; Powell-Harpstead Inc; Israel Berger & Associates

Terminus 200
Atlanta, USA

Completion Date: August 2009
Height to Architectural Top[1]: 113m (370ft)
Stories[1]: 25
Area: 79,664 sq m (857,496 sq ft)
Primary Use[1]: Office
Other Use: Retail
Owner/Developer: Cousins Properties Inc
Design Architect: Duda/Paine Architects LLP
Associate Architect: HKS Inc
Structural Engineer: Brockett/Davis/Drake Inc
MEP Engineer: Barrett, Woodyard and Associates Inc
Main Contractor: Hardin Construction
Other Consultants: HGOR Landscape Architects and Planners

Trump SoHo Hotel
New York, USA

Completion Date: April 2010
Height to Architectural Top[1]**:** 138m (454ft)
Stories[1]**:** 42
Area: 34,745 sq m (373,992 sq ft)
Primary Use[1]**:** Hotel
Owner: The Trump Organization; Bayrock Group LLC; The Sapir Organization
Developer: Bayrock Group LLC; The Sapir Organization
Design Architect: Handel Architects LLP
Structural Engineer: DeSimone Consulting Engineers
MEP Engineer: Cosentini Associates
Main Contractor: Bovis Lend Lease
Other Consultants: Israel Berger & Associates

Two Alliance Center
Atlanta, USA

Completion Date: July 2009
Height to Architectural Top[1]**:** 121m (395ft)
Stories[1]**:** 25
Area: 48,740 sq m (524,632 sq ft)
Primary Use[1]**:** Office
Owner/Developer: Tishman Speyer
Design Architect: Smallwood, Reynolds, Stewart, Stewart & Associates Inc
Structural Engineer: SDL Structural Engineers
MEP Engineer: AHA Consulting Engineers
Main Contractor: The Beck Group
Other Consultants: Mack Scogin Merrill Elam Architects

W Hoboken
Hoboken, USA

Completion Date: April 2009
Height to Architectural Top[1]**:** 96m (313ft)
Stories[1]**:** 27
Area: 25,958 sq m (279,410 sq ft)
Primary Use[1]**:** Mixed: Residential/Hotel
Owner/Developer: Ironstate Development Company
Design Architect: Gwathmey Siegel & Associates Architects LLC
Structural Engineer: Goldstein Associates PLLC
MEP Engineer: Cosentini Associates
Main Contractor: AJD Construction Company Inc
Other Consultants: LGA Engineering Inc; Melillo & Bauer; HDLC Architectural Lighting

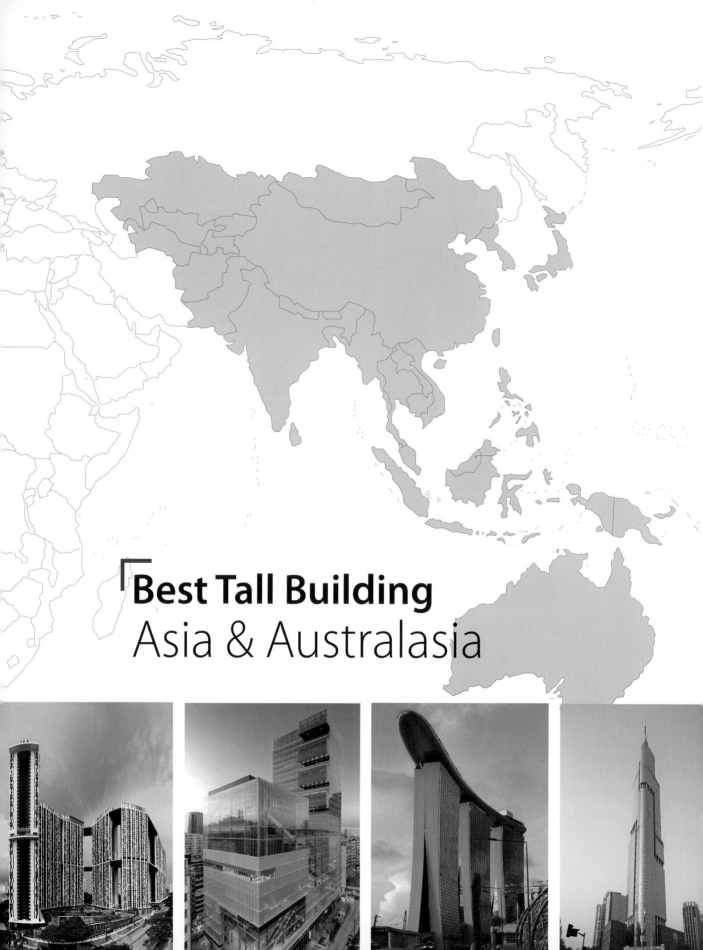

Best Tall Building
Asia & Australasia

Pinnacle @ Duxton

Singapore

The Pinnacle @ Duxton defines super-density housing with 1,848 apartment units built on a plot of only 2.5 hectares (6 acres)—only slightly larger than two football fields. Public housing as an architectural typology is inherently complex. It marries housing—the most private of programs—with public space. The public housing project addresses pragmatic, financial, social and even political issues. Add to that an irregular west facing site in the heart of Singapore's congested central business district, trees to be conserved and required connections to the neighboring park and community center, and the brief is incredibly complex.

The Pinnacle @ Duxton resolves these issues in an elegant manner and in the process creates a totally new aesthetic for public housing and typology for tall buildings. It boldly demonstrates a sustainable urban high-rise, high-density living and initiates an innovative typology of public communal spaces that are metaphorically reclaimed from the air. Seven tower blocks are placed in the most open and porous way, creating urban windows that frame the city skyline. With this maneuver, the layout eliminates overlooking between units; optimizes views, connection, air and light flow; minimizes western exposure to reduce solar heat gain; and includes the conservation of historical trees. A large forecourt for the towers was created, maintaining visual connectivity with the existing Tanjong Pagar Community Club, which is a major community node for this neighborhood.

Within the development, residents enjoy the convenience of shops, a food court, an education center, a childcare center, and two residents' committee centers. Beyond the development, residents are served by two train stations which link them to the island-wide mass rapid transit system and bus stops at the development's doorstep with a bus interchange depot. Exploiting the inherent sustainability of the high-density, high-rise housing model, The Pinnacle @ Duxton creates a walkable and diverse community, and provides a connected, convenient and compact model of sustainable urbanism.

On the ground, a new architectural surface warps, peels and flows over the carpark and services, efficiently organizing vehicular and pedestrian circulation. The linear block layout allows for a direct services network in the car park; a double-volume carriageway running under the blocks accommodates the fire engines and waste disposal. The peripheral arrangement of service cores allows for the car park to be efficiently and clearly laid out. The new architectural surface is a lush environmental deck that connects strategically with the existing urban network while forming a green lung for the city. Landscape elements comprising pavilion, benches, and exercise nodes are

Completion Date: December 2009
Height to Architectural Top[1]: 163m (536ft)
Stories[1]: 51
Area: 253,957 sq m (2,733,570 sq ft)
Primary Use[1]: Residential
Owner/Developer: Housing & Development Board, Singapore
Design Architect: ARC Studio Architecture + Urbanism
Associate Architect: RSP Architects Planners & Engineers Pte Ltd
Structural Engineer: Surbana International Consultants Pte Ltd
MEP Engineer: Surbana International Consultants Pte Ltd
Main Contractor: Chip Eng Seng Contractors (1988) Pte Ltd
Other Consultants: Envirospace Consultants Pte Ltd; T.Y. Lin International Pte Ltd

[1] For all definitions used in the data sections throughout this book, refer to CTBUH criteria shown on pages 184–187

Opposite: Overall view from Cantonment Road

"We are now finally seeing real movements towards the connected multi-level vertical city. The fact that the Pinnacle @ Duxton achieves this within a public housing scheme is remarkable."

Antony Wood, Juror, CTBUH

Left: 26th story sky garden
Opposite Top: 50th story sky garden
Opposite Bottom: Aerial view of 3rd story podium landscape

> **"A big step forward in rethinking residential design, this massive development manages to be light, highly efficient and well integrated with its surroundings."**
>
> *Ahmad Abdelrazaq, Juror, Samsung Corporation*

plug-ins to this extended park network and function as location markers as well as vibrant community nodes. Layers of tree screens border the site and pathways to provide varying degrees of opacity and privacy, softening the massiveness of the towers to create a human scale. Integrated within this landscape is an outdoor gallery, "Traces," which captures the historical significance of this site by tracing the outlines of the original two public housing blocks which were built in the 60s.

Continuous Sky Gardens on the 26th and 50th floors weave through the seven tower blocks, forming a simple yet powerful sculptural skyline that creates a strong identity for the project. Twelve Sky Gardens are conceptualized as displaced landscapes like a Sky Gym, Hillock, Crater, Meadows, Lounge, and Beach. They function as an extension of the living environment for residents, forming almost 1 hectare (2.5 acres) of new land. Designed with children playgrounds, an outdoor fitness gym for the elderly, landscape furniture resembling beach deck chairs and outdoor sofa sets; they provide diverse, creative and unusual spaces for community interaction. They also function as areas of refuge in case of emergencies and allow the sustainable sharing of mechanical services, reducing seven sets to just three. The seamless connection created by the linking sky bridges allow for the entire development to be serviced by a single Building Maintenance Unit.

Jury Statement

The Pinnacle @ Duxton is a large, dense development, but great effort was made towards the sustainable quality of life and sense of place on a project that otherwise may have become a relentless wall in the landscape. The project has enlivening spaces and creates a quality experience for the users. This building, as it curves across its site, takes the concept of "streets in the sky" to a new level, providing integrated public outdoor green spaces with its two linear sky parks. This provides a fascinating experiment in high density living and how we can make best use of that most precious of resources—land.

All the more impressive is that the project was able to accomplish such a high level of execution and the inclusion of so much public space within the constraints of a public housing project. Very rarely do you see such success in making a public housing project a clear architectural statement.

The individual apartment unit is designed with growth of the occupants in mind—from newly-weds to homes with kids, then teenagers and later grandchildren. The pre-cast flat slab system and structural column zoning allowed the flexibility of wall placement in lightweight concrete, which extends 400mm (15.7in) on either side of the grid—thus rooms can contract or expand to suit the occupants.

Efficiently constructed off-site, the pre-fabricated concrete building components were delivered and put together on-site. Residents were given an unprecedented choice of exterior façade treatments—planter boxes, bays, bay windows, windows, and balconies. The façade is atomized into modular panels strung together to form seven sets. Composed by simple rules, the layered sets form a complex façade. The pre-fabricated panels incorporate both structure and services—including columns, beams and service ducts. With a simple and affordable application of paint finish, a highly differentiated façade is created from an undifferentiated fabrication process—creating visual interest and reducing the perceived building mass.

Left: View from playground
Opposite: From top to bottom: Typical tower plan, 26th floor sky bridge plan, and 3rd floor podium plan

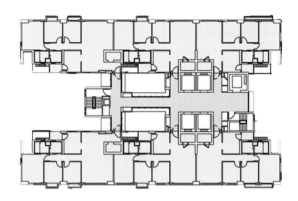

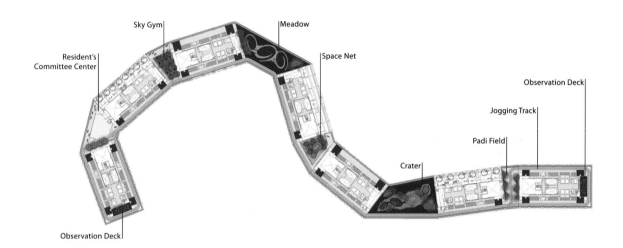

Sky Gym

Meadow

Resident's
Committee Center

Space Net

Observation Deck

Jogging Track

Padi Field

Crater

Observation Deck

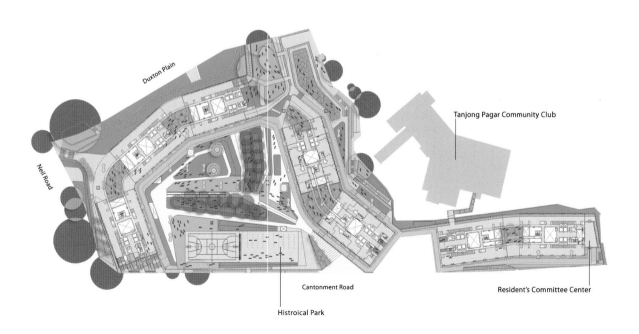

Duxton Plain

Tanjong Pagar Community Club

Neil Road

Cantonment Road

Histroical Park

Resident's Committee Center

iSQUARE

Hong Kong, China

Fluidity and transparency of the spatial arrangement were the emphasis of the design concept for iSQUARE. The program of the building has two major components—retail shops and restaurants. The new retail experience extends up the full height of the building through a series of sky-atria that orchestrate spatial tensions in stratifications within the space. The vibrant spatial energy, in perfect accord with the bustling but somewhat chaotic contextual character of this part of Tsim Sha Tsui, is likewise manifested on the strangled and dislocated external formal treatment of the tower that allows it to stand out in the congested skyline. Oddly shaped as it may seem, the form is generated entirely in response to contextual view angles, circulation arrangements, and the functional needs of the new design brief. By drawing in the public's participation into the architecture it permeates the public domain to the highest floors allowing the site to now assume an enhanced civic significance.

On the exterior, the two forces of fluidity and transparency are manifested through an interplay of a series of large volume glass boxes and escalator systems: the ground floor and first floor of the new building are occupied by double-story-high branded flagship shops with direct street access. A set of express escalators deliver visitors directly onto the second floor of the building—the Lobby Floor—where journeys to different destinations begin: a double volume Event Floor, Restaurant Floor, Cinema Boxes, and ultimately a 400-seat IMAX cinema, the largest in Hong Kong, floating in the sky at the top of the podium. All these express escalators are strategically placed along the Nathan Road façade as bridge connections to the various sky atria to echo the movement and dynamism in the bustling streets below.

At the top of the building, to capitalize on the breathtaking panoramic view of Victoria Harbor towards Hong Kong Island on the south, and also to positively respond to the blocky urban fabric at higher altitude, a 12-story tower housing most of the food and beverage outlets was planned and oriented for view optimization. Full-story-high vision glass panels at the three major façades have been allowed for at the tower. Balconies facing south are added to promote outdoor dining for the enjoyment of sunshine. In contrast to the tower element, where capitalization of harbor view is a major design direction, the podium portion of the building only reaches to a height similar with the existing adjoining buildings in the neighborhood, thus helping sustain continuity of the lower building line with a greater sense of urban block delineation.

For the podium, apart from the sky atria, a large portion of the podium façade is clad with a specially designed opaque curtain wall system integrated with warm white LED lights. This innovative lighting

Completion Date: December 2009
Height to Architectural Top[1]**:** 139m (456ft)
Stories[1]**:** 28
Area: 53,047 sq m (570,993 sq ft)
Primary Use[1]**:** Retail
Owner/Developer: Associated International Hotels Ltd
Design Architect: Rocco Design Architects Ltd
Structural Engineer: Meinhardt (Civil & Structural) Ltd
MEP Engineer: Meinhardt (M&E) Ltd
Main Contractor: Gammon Construction Ltd
Other Consultants: Meinhardt Façade Technology (HK) Ltd; Benoy Ltd; Davis Langdon & Seah Hong Kong Ltd

Opposite: Overall view from south east

84

"The transparency not only draws the public into the retail space, but, through the activity and movement within, reflects the busy dynamism that characterizes this part of Hong Kong."

Peter Murray, Juror, New London Architecture Centre

Left: Façade detail
Opposite Left: Street view from east
Opposite Right: Main sky-atrium escalators
Opposite Bottom Left: Lobby floor plan (top), typical floor plan (bottom)
Opposite Bottom Right: Section

> ## "The design excels at making a vibrant vertical city of retail shops by the strategic and careful planning of functional space and vertical circulation."
>
> *Bruce Kuwabara, Juror, KPMB Architects,*

scheme gives a unique glowing lantern effect which blends well with the existing neon-covered streetscape of Nathan Road at night and yet remains visually distinctive from the rest. LED lights were strategically chosen, instead of typical metal halide lighting, for reduced energy consumption.

Jury Statement

That we have now reached a 28-story tall retail mall says much about our consumer society; iSQUARE achieves this height with grace and transparency, rare of most retail buildings. The sky atria animate the building and draw visitors to the retail and restaurants which extend right to the top of the building. The setback of the podium and the creation of a new civic plaza is a welcome gesture in such a compact city.

The use of the curtain wall system with composite backpan incorporating thermal insulation at the podium not only creates a neat and tidy outlook to the new building (unlike other typical shopping malls), but also contributes to the reduction of cooling load. Similarly, for capturing the magnificent sea view, insulated glass units consisting of double low-E glass panes are adopted at the vision panels of the tower without increasing the burden on the air-conditioning system. In order to achieve a better energy efficiency result, water-cooled chillers have also been adopted for the centralized air-conditioning system of the new building for the higher coefficient of performance (COP) as compared to air-cooled chillers.

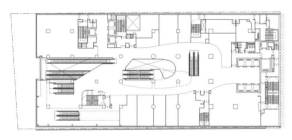

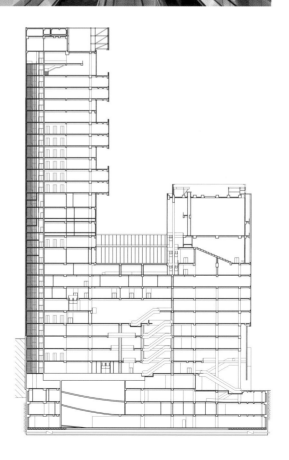

Marina Bay Sands Integrated Resort
Singapore

Marina Bay Sands is a high-density, mixed-use integrated resort that brings together a 2,560-room hotel, a SkyPark, convention center, shopping and dining, theaters, museum, and a casino across the water from Singapore's central business district. The 929,000 sq m (10,000,000 sq ft) urban district anchors the Singapore waterfront, and creates a gateway to Singapore. The design approach for the complex was not as a building project, but as a microcosm of a city—rooted in Singapore's culture, climate and contemporary life. The aim was to create an urban landscape capable of addressing the issue of megascale.

The project is designed as an urban structure that weaves together the components of a complex program into a dynamic urban crossroads and public meeting place. Inspired by great ancient cities that were ordered around a vital public thoroughfare, Marina Bay Sands is organized around two principal axes that traverse the district and give it a sense of orientation placing emphasis on the pedestrian street as the focus of civic life. Combining indoor and outdoor spaces and providing a platform for a wide array of activities, this vibrant, 21st-century *cardo maximus*, or grand arcade, also connects to the subway and other transportation. A series of layered gardens provide ample green space throughout the site, extending the tropical garden landscape from Marina City Park towards the Bayfront. The landscape network reinforces urban connections with the resort's surroundings and every level of the district has green space that is accessible to the public.

The most innovative aspect of Marina Bay Sands, both conceptually and technically, is the 1 hectare (2.5 acre) SkyPark atop the hotel towers. Locating the park and hotel amenities at 200m (656ft) above the sea afforded the architect the ability to keep the majority of the project relatively low in height. The three 55-story hotel towers anchor the district and are connected at the top by the SkyPark—an engineering marvel that, at 340m (1,115ft), is longer than the Eiffel Tower is tall and large enough to park four-and-a-half A380 jumbo jets. The 65m (213ft) cantilever of the SkyPark past the third hotel tower forms one of the world's largest public cantilevers.

The SkyPark accommodates a public observatory, gardens, a 151 meter-long (495 foot-long) swimming pool, restaurants, and jogging paths and offers sweeping panoramic views, a formidable resource in a dense city like Singapore. Shielded from the winds and lavishly planted with hundreds of trees, the SkyPark celebrates the notion of the Garden City that has been the underpinning of Singapore's urban design strategy.

Completion Date: June 2010
Height to Architectural Top[1]: 207m (679ft)
Stories[1]: 57
Area: 249,843 sq m (2,689,288 sq ft)
Primary Use[1]: Hotel
Owner/Developer: Marina Bay Sands Pte Ltd (a subsidiary of the Las Vegas Sands Corporation)
Design Architect: Safdie Architects
Associate Architect: Aedas Ltd
Structural Engineer: Arup
MEP Engineer: R.G. Vanderweil, LLP
Main Contractor: Ssangyong
Other Consultants: Parsons Brinckerhoff Pte Ltd; Peter Walker & Partners Landscape Architects; Hirsch Bender Associates; CL3

Opposite: Overall view of the hotel towers and high level SkyPark

"The unique SkyPark is an instant icon for the city and has the potential to do for Singapore what the Sydney Opera House did for Sydney."

Mun Summ Wong, Juror, WOHA Architects

Left: View from Marina Bay
Opposite Top Left: Interior lobby view
Opposite Top Right: Interior atrium view
Opposite Bottom: Typical floor plans and SkyPark plan

"Bringing the SkyPark into the sky—a floating ship-like structure that overlooks the seas—is a remarkable feat of engineering."

Ahmad Abdelrazaq, Juror, Samsung Corporation

A post-tensioned box girder was designed to achieve this incredible cantilever. The maximum depth of the box girder is 10m (33ft) at the end support from the hotel tower and generally 3.5m (11ft) deep. The lifting of the SkyPark was one of the many challenges that the project faced that required an innovative approach to the construction methods in order to facilitate one of the highest strand jacking operations ever undertaken.

The hotel towers on which the SkyPark sits has an unusual and spectacular form that creates its distinct silhouette. Each tower is formed by two curved and splayed legs that lean into one another as they rise, ultimately becoming one at the upper levels. At the ground level, the space between each tower is enclosed to create a hotel lobby and atrium, at the upper levels the space is conceived as an "urban window" that allows for views through the project. Major steel trusses form a connection between the separate segments of the building's legs to provide a frame to transfer sheer between the towers and tie the buildings together to resist lateral forces.

Jury Statement

The curved and sweeping legs of the three hotel towers that rise up to culminate in a continuous bridging SkyPark anchor its site at the gateway to Singapore's harbor with a strong and highly iconic structure. The engineering and planning that went into the SkyPark's construction and incredible cantilever are commendable, as is the bringing of amenity and green spaces to the top of the towers, allowing further open space at grade.

90

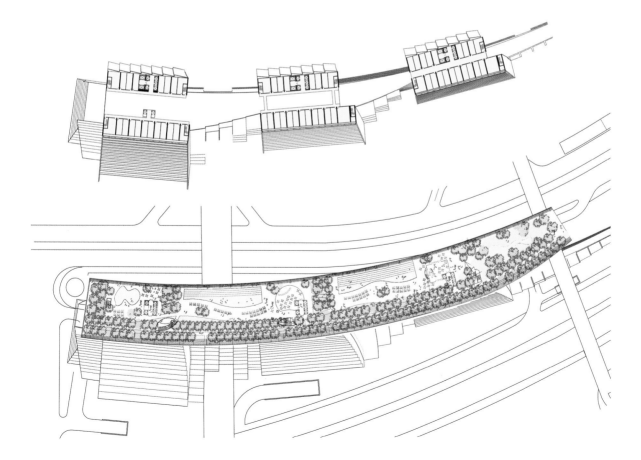

Nanjing Greenland Financial Center
Nanjing, China

Nanjing Greenland Financial Center is a mixed-use complex comprising of several buildings resting on two sites, parcels A1 and A2. Parcel A1 contains a podium connecting two towers. The taller 450m (1,476ft) tower consists of offices and hotels, and the 100m (328ft) tower contains purely office space. The shape and placement of the buildings are designed to echo the geometry of the existing roads and maximize exterior views of the city. The buildings' composition maintains the east–west viewing corridors along East Beijing Road and provides a visual link to the nearby historical drum and bell towers.

Landscaping is a significant part of the complex as the buildings are set back from the street with several large landscaped, public open spaces. South of parcel A1, is a sunken garden that will connect to the future subway. There is also a roof garden at the top of the podium in parcel A1 to reduce the heat island effect. In addition to the ground level and podium garden spaces, the design incorporates sky gardens that wind their way up the façade, bringing the green all the way up the tower.

Completion Date: February 2010
Height to Architectural Top[1]: 450m (1,476ft)
Stories[1]: 66
Area: 137,529 sq m (1,480,350 sq ft)
Primary Use[1]: Mixed: Hotel/Office
Developer: Nanjing State Owned Assets & Greenland Financial Center Co Ltd
Design Architect: Skidmore, Owings & Merrill LLP
Associate Architect: ECADI
Structural Engineer: Skidmore, Owings & Merrill LLP
MEP Engineer: Skidmore, Owings & Merrill LLP
Main Contractor: Shanghai Construction Group
Other Consultants: Lerch Bates & Associates; The RJA Group, Inc; RWDI, Inc; STS Consultants; SWA Group

As one of the tallest structures in the world to date (ranked as the sixth tallest building in the world at the time of its completion by the CTBUH) and being constructed in a seismic region, enhanced design measures and performance-based evaluations were utilized in order to obtain seismic review approval for the main tower. The critical parts of the lateral system were designed for earthquake forces between two and six times more than typically required by Chinese code. Additionally, a full 3-Dimensional Non-Linear Elasto-Plastic analysis for a 2,500-year earthquake was completed to determine the structural response and serviceability. A multi-stage axial shortening, creep and shrinkage analysis was also performed to evaluate the long-term load sharing between the central core and the perimeter of the Tower through the outrigger truss system.

The tower features a unique façade system, rather than a typical flush-glass curtain wall system; it is composed of offset modular panels that protrude in plan to create a distinctive texture to the building's elevations. Each curtain wall unit is a triangle in plan and shifts a half module between each two floors. It creates a scaled effect and has a very unique visual appeal in catching the light and reflections of the city. The small edge of the triangle unit is a fixed perforated metal panel with a hidden operable panel behind it for natural ventilation and smoke exhaust. This will help to reduce mechanical ventilation energy usage during some transitional seasons. The long edge of each triangle unit consists of a high performance insulated low-E glass panel, to help to cut down the heat gain through the building façade.

Opposite: Overall view from the south east

"For a tower that was the sixth tallest in the world at completion this building has received little attention. The skillful handling of the serrated façade alone makes that a travesty."

Antony Wood, Juror, CTBUH

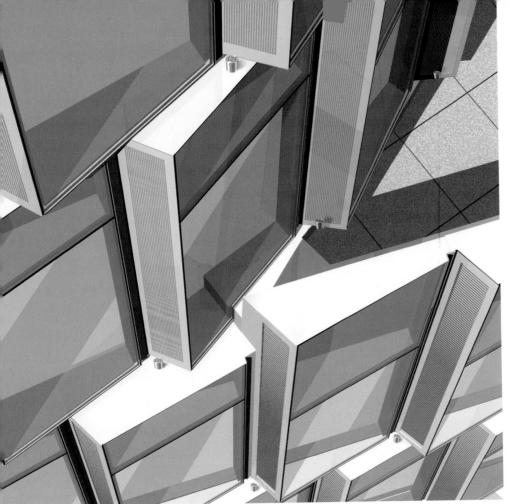

The office tower is served by floor-by-floor, variable volume, supply air handling units with variable speed drive. Four pipe fan coil units are provided for hotel guest rooms. Gas fired steam boilers and chillers, and associated water pumps are located on the first basement level. Gas service is brought into the building for the boilers and for kitchens. The fire protection system for the building consists of a zoned combination automatic sprinkler and standpipe system in accordance with regulatory requirements for a fully sprinklered high-rise building in China.

The office tower is served by two banks of seven elevators, one bank for the low-rise office levels, and one for the high-rise office levels. Two service elevators are designated as fire elevators and serve all floors of the office tower (three separate service elevators will serve all floors of the hotel). The hotel portion of the main tower will be served by three express passenger elevators from the ground floor entrance lobby to the level 36 sky lobby, where five local passenger lifts will take guests up to the highest hotel level on 65.

Jury Statement

The triangulated, serrated façade treatment is interesting, adding depth and texture to the imposing form while allowing natural ventilation throughout. Carefully sited and planned, the tower creates a "flatiron" effect—stretched to its incredible height—on one of Nanjing's busiest intersections.

94

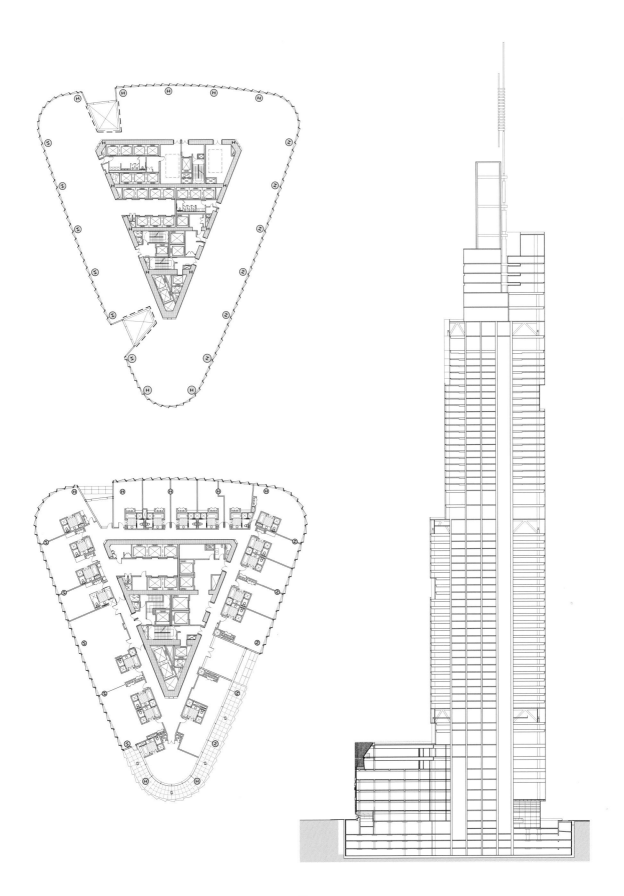

Northeast Asia Trade Tower
Incheon, South Korea

The Northeast Asia Trade Tower (NEATT) symbolizes the region's role as a new center of economic activity and development. The tower embodies the planning principles of New Songdo City, a 607 hectare (1,500 acre), master-planned community on the Incheon, Korea, waterfront. NEATT is a large-scale mixed-use development designed to attract top tier Global and Korean companies as tenants to this new international free-trade zone. Occupying a site centrally located at the southern edge of Songdo Central Park, the tower is adjacent to the Songdo Convensia Convention Center, and near the Songdo First World Towers. The tallest building in Korea at the time of its completion, NEATT rises above the new city offering views of the Yellow Sea, the cities of Seoul and Incheon, and the surrounding mountains.

The tall form tapers from a trapezoid shape at the ground level to a triangle at the top, reflecting the shifting programs within. The tower's large base accommodates the open floor plates required by office tenants, while the tower's slender upper floors provide hotel and residential spaces with shallower floor plates, maximizing views and light penetration. The very top of the tower—its observation space—is fittingly paired with the tower's most slender profile. The transition in plan from trapezoidal to triangular form translates into an elegant exterior with reflective faces that resemble elongated triangles, the edges of which converge and diverge in an alternating pattern.

The form appears to lean toward Songdo Central Park and, in fact, it does bow out by 5m (16ft). This effect is achieved without compromising the tower's stability. To stabilize the structure of the building, the core rises vertically and the centroid of the tower mass aligns with the centroid of the tower ground level, thereby eliminating any rotational forces in the foundation from the tower form. This results in a very efficient structural system. The concrete core and the lightweight steel floor framing are conventional construction methods resulting in a cost effective building.

NEATT serves as a model of sustainable design strategies, carefully balancing energy conservation, increased indoor environmental quality, and occupant comfort. The exterior glazing allows for abundant daylight penetration and expansive views. Exterior shading devices, together with a high performance glazing specification, limit solar heat gain and reduce air conditioning costs. Operable windows allow for smoke exhaust and small LED lights are embedded into the façade outriggers greatly reducing the energy spent on lighting the building at night.

Like other buildings in New Songdo City, NEATT purchases district hot water from a new, highly

Completion Date: June 2010
Height to Architectural Top[1]: 305m (1,001ft)
Stories[1]: 68
Area: 140,000 sq m (1,506,947 sq ft)
Primary Use[1]: Mixed: Residential/Hotel/Office
Other Use: Retail
Owner/Developer: Gale International
Design Architect: Kohn Pedersen Fox Associates
Associate Architect: Heerim Architects
Structural Engineer: Arup; Dongyang Structural
MEP Engineer: Arup
Main Contractor: Daewoo

Opposite: Overall view from Songdo Central Park

"Despite its seemingly complex geometry, the structural design concept is well integrated into the architecture."

Ahmad Abdelrazaq, Juror, Samsung Corporation

Left: Façade detail showing tower louvers
Opposite Left: Axonometric of tower
Opposite Right: From top to bottom: 65th, 36th, and 2nd floor plans

> "NEATT stands sentinel at the head of the new Songdo Park. More than this, the project is testimony to the incredible urban achievement that is the New Songdo."
>
> *Antony Wood, Juror, CTBUH*

efficient cogeneration facility located nearby. Hot water, used for heating and cooling via absorption chillers, is generated from waste heat recovered during the process of producing electricity. The building is estimated to reduce source-energy CO_2 emissions by 6,000 tons per year when compared to a "standard" code-compliant office tower with on-site electric chillers and a natural-gas boiler plant.

Because water conservation is a chief concern in Korea, the design for NEATT addresses this issue in several ways. First, low-flow plumbing fixtures reduce water usage by more than 20% in comparison to the consumption rate of a typical office building. Second, a grey water collection system is used for flushing toilets and urinals to further decrease potable water demand and reduce sewage conveyance. Third, the building utilizes collected stormwater for site irrigation via large storage tanks, reducing potable water used for this purpose by more than 50%.

Jury Statement

Northeast Asia Trade Tower's tapering form is well suited for its mixed-use program, creating large floor plates at the base for office function, smaller floor areas higher up for hotel, then residential—a beautiful solution to the changing programmatic needs of the ever increasingly common mixed-use towers. Holding a prominent presence in the New Songdo City skyline, the tower anchors what is an all new community as an extension of the city of Incheon.

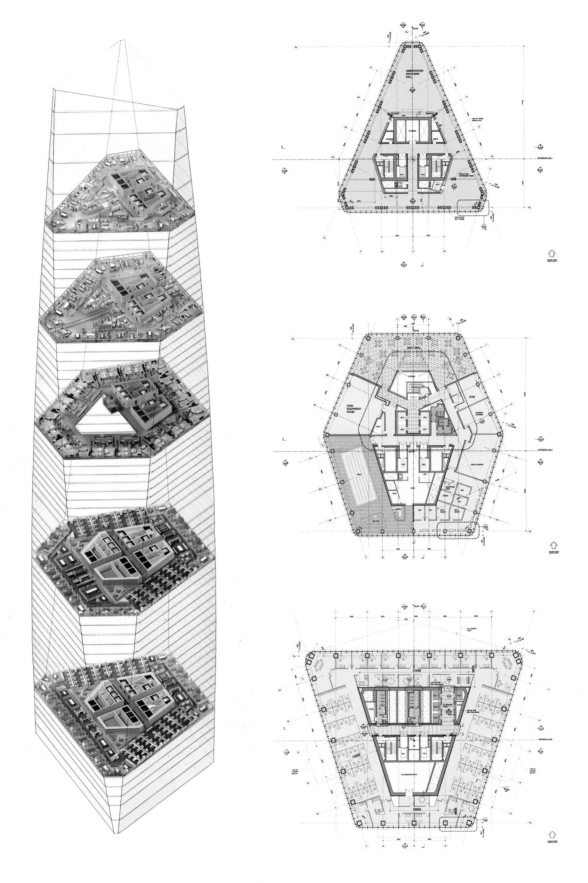

400 George Street
Brisbane, Australia

Recognizing that cities are dominated by office buildings in which corporate foyers, of limited public value or interest, consume much of the urban ground plane, this project shifts the typology of office towers from corporate institutions to public realms. In 400 George Street, the visitor experience is one of entering an "urban room", a retreat from the city immersed in art. The space reveals the greater public invitation of accessible facilities, particularly an elevated food hall extending along and cantilevering over the entire George Street frontage, but also a full-time child care center and a series of social spaces.

The architectural form directly reinforces this ethos, sculpturally reaching out to the streetscapes at the base, and rising through increasingly calmer segments to the rooftop garden. These segments modulate the façades while responding environmentally to the tower's climatic context, the responses and innovations being principal reasons for the selection of 400 George Street as the new home of the Queensland Government's Department of Environment and Natural Resources.

Completion Date: October 2009
Height to Architectural Top[1]: 150m (492ft)
Stories[1]: 37
Area: 51,549 sq m (554,869 sq ft)
Primary Use[1]: Office
Owner/Developer: Grosvenor Australia Investments Pty Ltd; Leighton Properties Pty Ltd
Design Architect: Cox Rayner Architects
Structural Engineer: Robert Bird Group
MEP Engineer: George Floth Pty Ltd
Main Contractor: Thiess Pty Ltd

Top: View of north east façade
Bottom: Street view
Opposite Top Left: 2nd floor plan
Opposite Bottom Left: Typical floor plan
Opposite Right: Turbot Street elevation

Through the tower, 400 George Street comprises significant combined innovations including a high performance glass panel façade system which is subtly modulated and subdued given the historic context of George Street, Brisbane. A key environmental innovation was the combination of the condensate recovery and condensate pump energy optimization systems. These optimization systems have been calculated to save 700,000 liters of water, 110,000 kwh of electrical energy and 100,000 kg of CO_2 over conventional towers of comparable size. The condensate recovery system harvests water from the air handling units,

while the condensate pump energy optimization controls the flow rate of condenser water through the chillers.

400 George Street illustrates how an office tower can contribute harmoniously to the high-rise context of the city without demanding visual attention, at the same time offering radical revision of the physical and social contribution that towers can make to the vitality of a city.

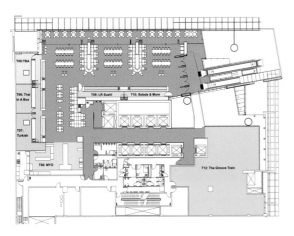

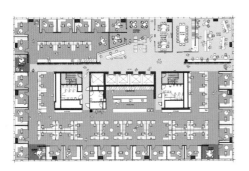

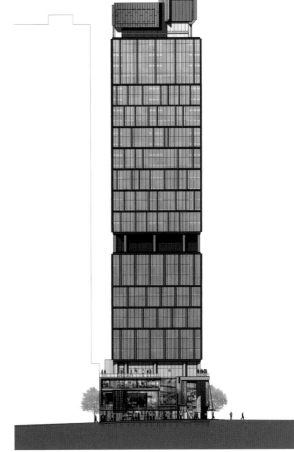

BEA Financial Tower
Shanghai, China

BEA Financial Tower development is a grade-A office building situated in a prominent location within the Lu Jia Zui commercial and financial district of Shanghai's Pudong. The tower sits next to the Jin Mao Building and the World Financial Center beside the Yang-Pu river and therefore is highly visible along the Pudong skyline directly from the Bund.

The building footprint responds to the boundary requirements by breaking down the built volumes programmatically into two wedge-shaped entities: the tower block and the low-rise building which is dedicated to restaurants, public facilities and support services. A glazed atrium separates the tower from the low-rise podium; the atrium and the low-rise are staggered volumetrically away from the tower's northwestern façade.

The tower is composed of a central circulation and service core which is flanked by two floor plates. The depth of the floor plates were carefully designed to allow natural light to all office space within. The west wing of the building rises above the other two

Completion Date: January 2009
Height to Architectural Top[1]: 198m (650ft)
Stories[1]: 42
Area: 70,000 sq m (753,474 sq ft)
Primary Use[1]: Office
Owner/Developer: Gaopeng (Shanghai) Real Estate Development Co Ltd
Design Architect: TFP Farrells Limited
Associate Architect: ECADI
Structural Engineer: ECADI
MEP Engineer: ECADI
Main Contractor: Shanghai No. 7 Construction Co Ltd
Other Consultants: KWP Ltd (Beijing); Arup Hong Kong

Top: Overall view
Bottom: Façade detail showing vertical fins
Opposite Left: Typical floor plan
Opposite Right: Sky garden section

components creating a stepped effect to bring a level of clarity and directness to the building's massing. Each element functions independently but is bound into a singular composition by complementary materials and modularity. A sense of the greenery being swept vertically into the building is captured by positioning sky gardens on the various refuge floors and creating a visual link to the park from ground level upwards.

Optimizing city and river views on the north sides whilst minimizing glare required a façade design composed of large areas of glazing with vertical fins that use a surface frit to shade the interior from low-glare sun angles. As well as producing an elongating effect, the fins add visual interest and depth to the façade and allows for special night lighting effects. Overall, four different types of cladding were established in order to minimize solar gain and building heat load on the south west and south. Where the percentage of glazed areas is reduced, horizontal shading devices are provided and low-E glass is used. Each type of cladding is designed to deal with specific environmental aspects: reducing solar gain, reducing glare, mitigating winter heat loss and maximizing aspect.

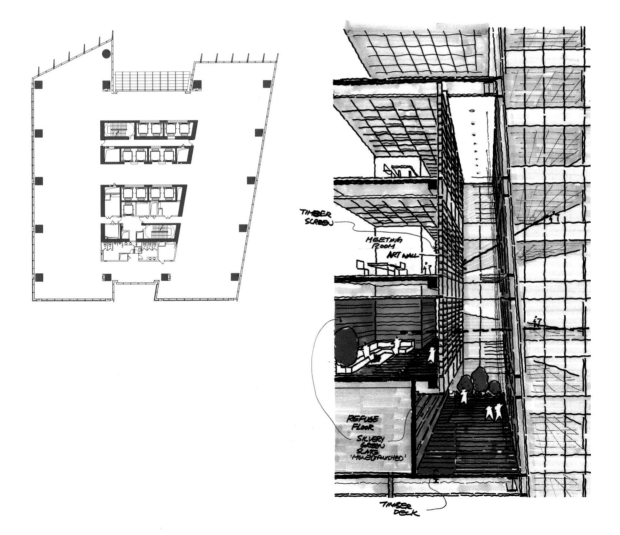

BUMPS
Beijing, China

Located in the Chaoyang District of Beijing, BUMPS integrates residential and commercial space in a square-shaped layout revolved 45 degrees off Beijing's cardinal axis. The rotation allows the building density to exceed 350% from Beijing's traditional north–south oriented residential buildings. In addition, the 45-degree angle allows the building to secure direct sunlight and stunning views from all individual flats.

BUMPS is made up of four residential towers, as well as a commercial complex. Every two floors are set as a "boxed" unit staggered 2m (6.5ft) horizontally, and the façade repeats the staggered spacing. The staggering of the units creates multiple setbacks, which are utilized for terraces and a restaurant on the sixth story of one of the commercial buildings. The interlaced black and white units highlight the concave–convex façade. Square glazed and louver windows are embedded into exterior walls in a stochastic layout. By randomly placing the windows across the façade, the existence of all pillars and beams is weakened, and the appearance of the buildings look stacked in small

Completion Date: February 2009
Height to Architectural Top[1]: 82m (269ft)
Stories[1]: 26
Area: 103,218 sq m (1,111,029 sq ft)
Primary Use[1]: Residential
Other Use: Retail
Owner: Beijing Xinfengxinde Real-Estate Development Co Ltd; Beijing Zihexin Plaza Co Ltd
Developer: Beijing Xinfengxinde Real-Estate Development Co Ltd
Design Architect: SAKO Architects
Structural Engineer: Beijing New Era Architectural Design Ltd
MEP Engineer: Beijing New Era Architectural Design Ltd
Main Contractor: Jiangsu Suzhong Construction Group Co Ltd

Top: Façade detail
Bottom: Overall view from West 4th Ring Road
Opposite Top Left: Typical residential floor plan
Opposite Bottom Left: Massing Diagram
Opposite Right: Typical tower section

black and white "boxes." The interior is equally geometric, continuing the exterior black and white theme, but also showing off the building's reinforced concrete construction and stonewalls. These walls are enhanced with carefully planned lighting and interior design, which adds to the energy of the architectural expression.

While tall buildings traditionally emphasize their verticality, BUMPS emphasizes the horizontal. Incorporating staggered terraces into the eight floor commercial buildings, and cantilevering the beams 9m (30ft) from the façade, the horizontal emphasis clearly displays the buildings dynamic function.

BUMPS does not merge with the local surroundings. It deliberately differentiates, standing as a landmark leading the development of the Chaoyang District. The staggered black and white "boxes" paired with changing window layouts exudes an energetic and dynamic visual. The crisp black and white units showcase the striking stacked cantilevers from the base to the very top.

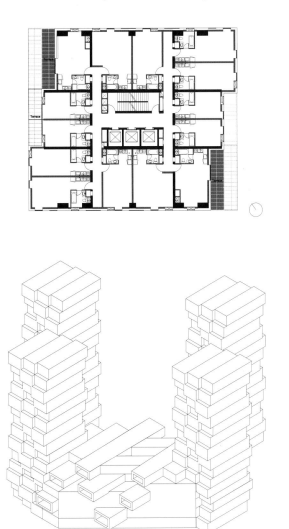

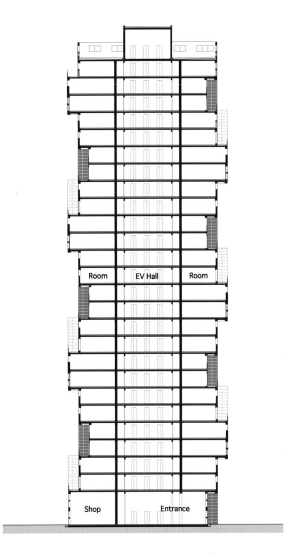

China Diamond Exchange Center
Shanghai, China

Providing space for members of the China Diamond Exchange, as well as other related and speculative tenants on the upper floors, the building also includes retail on the ground floor and a second floor that features the elevator lobby, exhibition space and a restaurant. The major tenants' core business inspired the design, with diamond-shaped elements featured throughout. References are seen most prominently in the atrium's glass skylight, the structural geometry of the entry canopy, and the main lobby floor.

The building is conceived as two rectangular office slabs connected by a sky-lit atrium, with a large, 20m x 70 m (66ft x 230ft) cable-supported net wall at each end. One tower is fully dedicated to the Diamond Exchange members and designed to provide them with secure transport from their below-grade parking spaces to their offices above. The adjacent tower serves the other tenants, with access through an open elevator tower in the center of the atrium. The elevator tower defines the focal point of the building, with three cabs traversing the atrium to sky bridges on each level that connect the two office blocks.

Completion Date: October 2009
Height to Architectural Top[1]: 77m (251ft)
Stories[1]: 15
Area: 49,750 sq m (535,505 sq ft)
Primary Use[1]: Office
Owner/Developer: Shanghai Lujiazui Development Co Ltd
Design Architect: Goettsch Partners
Associate Architect: Shanghai Zhong-fu Architects
Structural Engineer: Shanghai Tong-qing Technologic Development Co Ltd
MEP Engineer: Shanghai Zhong-fu Architects
Main Contractor: Shanghai No. 2 Construction Co Ltd
Other Consultants: ADI Limited; Shanghai New Century Co Ltd

Top: Overall view
Bottom: Interior atrium and skylight with open elevator tower

Crown Hotel at City of Dreams
Macau, China

The City of Dreams is a new 380,000 sq m (4,000,000 sq ft) resort casino development on the Cotai strip in Macau. The Crown hotel is the tallest of four hotel towers within the project, each of which was designed to have its own distinct identity while their architectural language ties them together as one coherent composition by means of using similar curtain wall materials, façade lighting and soft flowing forms, which respond to the water elements within and around the project. The Crown Hotel's elliptical tower rises from the expansive series of reflecting pools and water features that define the main frontage of the project along the Cotai strip. A series of vertical façade fins descend from the top of the tower breaking up as they reach the reflecting pools at the base, reminiscent of falling rain.

The Crown tower followed a "Jump Start" construction. Steel structural framing was quickly erected up to the first typical hotel floor to enable an early start on the repetitive concrete framed typical floors using system form work. This enabled the more complex non-typical steel framed podium floors to be constructed concurrently with the tower.

Completion Date: March 2009
Height to Architectural Top[1]: 151m (495ft)
Stories[1]: 36
Area: 69,000 sq m (742,710 sq ft)
Primary Use[1]: Hotel
Owner/Developer: Melco Crown Entertainment Limited
Design Architect: Arquitectonica
Associate Architect: Leigh & Orange
Structural Engineer: Mott Connell Ltd
MEP Engineer: J Roger Preston Limited
Main Contractor: Leighton-China State-John Holland, JV
Other Consultants: Bates Smart; Arup Fire Hong Kong

Top: Overall night view
Bottom: Hotel room interior

Deloitte Centre

Auckland, New Zealand

This building is a site specific response to the existing Auckland central business district context, and to the history of this sacred Maori site which was once a fertile river valley that flowed into the Waitemata Harbor. The building embraces a material strategy to acknowledge the former location of the land/sea edge, and to create an "anchor" to recall the former location of the harbor.

The building has been designed to respond to the variable scale of context of the whole city block. This is achieved by the podium being scaled and articulated to both the width of the adjacent streets and the height of the buildings on the opposite side of the street. Many are identified as historic buildings of their period and the boundary alignment of such a collection of buildings becomes a significant urban design and streetscape determinant. Thus the podium was developed to ensure the special character of this heritage precinct in downtown Auckland is respected and revitalized. The overall massing of the building is comprised of vertical sliding gestures that emphasize the building height, reference the most important intersection in the city and playfully recall the

Completion Date: December 2009
Height to Architectural Top[1]: 96m (316ft)
Stories[1]: 21
Area: 36,795 sq m (396,058 sq ft)
Primary Use[1]: Office
Owner/Developer: Brookfield Multiplex NZ
Design Architect: Woods Bagot
Associate Architect: Warren and Mahoney
Structural Engineer: Holmes Consulting Group
MEP Engineer: Norman Disney & Young
Main Contractor: Brookfield Multiplex NZ
Other Consultants: Aurecon; Rider Levett Bucknell; Holmes Fire; Dave Pearson Architects Limited; MPC Planning; Tonkin & Taylor; Light Works

Top: Overall view from south west
Bottom: Building entry
Opposite Left: Façade detail at south elevation
Opposite Right: Typical section

previous alignment of Auckland's Harbor. In addition to these broad moves, a finer scale is achieved by a varied use of façade materials and articulation that respond to orientation. A triple skin on the west elevation with automatic louvers regulates airflow through the cavity and creates a highly transparent façade.

Winter gardens distributed over six levels create interconnecting voids that animate the podium spaces to deliver a high performance work place. The two tenants in this building—the Bank of New Zealand and Deloitte Ltd—have very different work styles. To most effectively accommodate these two work styles, the building shifts from a large floor plate central core building at podium level to an offset/end core in smaller floors through the tower. This shift in floor plate configuration was achieved while also avoiding any structural transfers.

The Deloitte Centre is a pilot project for the introduction of the New Zealand Green Building Council rating system. This building is the most environmentally sustainable commercial office building in New Zealand and pioneered the development of the system.

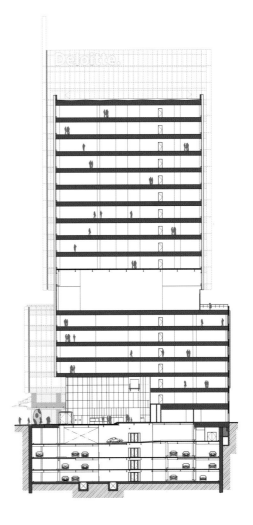

MOSAIC

Beijing, China

Originally conceived as an office building over a department store, construction halted when the structural frame reached the fourth level and sat abandoned for many years. Following the renovation and conversion of the unfinished building, MOSAIC's program changed to three residential towers over a large retail podium.

The motif of "mosaic" was adopted throughout this project to convey the image of a landmark filled with festivity—like the spectacle of fluttering confetti. The façades are composed of six shades of purple and white painted panels, translucent glass windows, and three colors of aluminum louvers. Each color was used on a simple regular pattern, yet it seems to be a random mosaic pattern in the context of the entire façade. The motif continues throughout the interior design and even through to the landscaping. The ground floor and the fifth floor roof garden utilize three types of grey stones, wood deck, and various plants, trees and grasses to carry out this "mosaic" aesthetic.

Completion Date: May 2009
Height to Architectural Top[1]: 97m (318ft)
Stories[1]: 23
Area: 100,359 sq m (1,080,255 sq ft)
Primary Use[1]: Residential
Other Use: Retail
Developer: Beijing Guo Rong Real Estate Development Ltd
Design Architect: SAKO Architects
Main Contractor: Qingdao Construction Group Co

Top: Overall view of towers in context
Bottom: Glass atrium ceiling with one of the towers visible beyond

NHN Green Factory
Seongnam, South Korea

As a young internet company, communication and change are the most important considerations in NHN's corporate image and work as the most important concept in the design of their new headquarters building. Wide open layouts in typical floor plans and communication zones on the fourth floor were designed to foster better communication and integration among employees.

The louvers placed on the façade create the overall image for the building. The louvers, which operate individually, convey a feeling of a canvas that constantly changes the building's front façade to represent the image of the continually changing young company. The west façade is planned as the main façade to convey the corporate image to a far distance, as the building can be easily recognized from the express highways to the west. Further, the whole building can be used for events by attaching pictures on the louvers to transform the building into an art box. From a practical standpoint, the integrated vertical louvers also provide a pleasant working environment by controlling the sunshine and shade to individual user comforts.

Top: View of west façade
Bottom: Interior common space with louvered perimeter walls

Completion Date: February 2010
Height to Architectural Top[1]: 134m (441ft)
Stories[1]: 28
Area: 101,662 sq m (1,094,281 sq ft)
Primary Use[1]: Office
Owner: NHN Corporation
Design Architect: Samoo Architects & Engineers; NBBJ
Structural Engineer: Kyungjai Structural Engineers
MEP Engineer: Samoo Electrical Consultant; Sunjin Mechanical Consultant; Arup
Main Contractor: Hyundai Engineering & Construction
Other Consultants: Saegil E&C; Soltos; Han Bang UBIS Co; Sunrex; Protek

Santos Place
Brisbane, Australia

Brisbane is a fast growing warm climate city with a relatively concentrated central business district surrounded by spacious suburbs. With the city's vivid light and raffish character, this plush commercial building in Brisbane is exuberant, tactile and colorful. Gold anodizing and the local heritage color palette give the façade a characteristic glow achievable in Brisbane's intense light, a homage to Australia's exuberant north. Double glazing on the perimeter is shielded by purposefully perforated shadowing screens on its west and east elevations.

The site has no real street frontage yet enjoys panoramic city and river views. The insertion of a laneway from Turbot to Tank Street unlocks this potential by providing a more fitting ground level address for a large commercial building. The ground level creates a people-friendly setting that signals a less corporate way of developing the city. Bicycle parking, boulder walls for sitting, and dangling lanterns suggest that an alternative gentleness might accompany big buildings rather than the singular splendor of massive glass and gleaming stainlessness.

Completion Date: March 2009
Height to Architectural Top[1]: 159m (522ft)
Stories[1]: 38 Stories
Area: 43,195 sq m (464,947 sq ft)
Primary Use[1]: Office
Other Use: Retail
Owner/Developer: Nielson Properties
Design Architect: Donovan Hill
Structural Engineer: Alliance Design Group
MEP Engineer: Lincolne Scott
Main Contractor: Hutchinson Builders
Other Consultants: Resource Coordination Partnership; Rider Levett Bucknall; Norman Disney & Young; Ron Rumble; Gamble McKinnon Green; KFM Partnership; Butler Partners

Above: Aerial view

Songdo First World Towers

Incheon, South Korea

First World Towers is the first residential development to be realized in New Songdo City, an all-new sustainable community in a free-trade zone on the waterfront in Incheon, Korea. Housing 7,000 of the city's 65,000 residents, First World Towers contains 2,545 apartments and live/work spaces, as well as a health club, a daycare center, and a senior's center.

The complex was conceived as being an assemblage of distinct communities. An analysis of Korean social hierarchy (the Ma-Ul, the Dong-Ne, and the Yi-Woot) informed the organization of the First World Towers into four courtyard communities each of which is subdivided into three neighborhoods of approximately 200 households. The traditional Korean built environment also influenced the design, wherein circulation through palaces and gardens is characterized by repeated shifts in orientation and displaced axes. At the perimeter, gates and seven-story street walls provide a sense of enclosure, beyond which densely planted interior courtyards are viewed through large scale "urban windows."

Top: Overall view from Central Park Lake
Bottom: Courtyard water feature

Completion Date: July 2009
Height to Architectural Top[1]**:** 237m (776ft)
Stories[1]**:** 67
Area: 531,606 sq m (5,722,159 sq ft)
Primary Use[1]**:** Residential
Owner/Developer: Gale International
Design Architect: Kohn Pedersen Fox Associates
Associate Architect: Kunwon Architect
Structural Engineer: Thornton Tomasetti
MEP Engineer: Cosentini Associates
Main Contractor: POSCO Engineering & Construction Co Ltd
Other Consultants: Towers/Golde

39 Conduit Road
Hong Kong, China

Completion Date: September 2009
Height to Architectural Top[1]: 191m (626ft)
Stories[1]: 42
Area: 18,266 sq m (196,614 sq ft)
Primary Use[1]: Residential
Owner: Nation Sheen Ltd & Carry Express Investment Ltd
Developer: Henderson Land Development Co Ltd; Peterson Holdings Co Ltd
Design Architect: Dennis Lau & Ng Chun Man Architects and Engineers (HK) Ltd
Structural Engineer: Stephen Cheng Consulting Engineers Ltd
MEP Engineer: Arup Hong Kong
Main Contractor: Heng Shung Construction Co Ltd
Other Consultants: AXXA Group Ltd

City Square Residences
Singapore

Completion Date: June 2009
Height to Architectural Top[1]: 104m (342ft)
Stories[1]: 30
Area: 22,379 sq m (240,886 sq ft)
Primary Use[1]: Residential
Owner/Developer: City Developments Ltd
Design Architect: Ong & Ong Pte Ltd
Structural Engineer: Meinhardt (Singapore) Pte Ltd
MEP Engineer: Parsons Brinckerhoff Pte Ltd
Main Contractor: Woh Hup Pte Ltd

Kalpataru Towers
Mumbai, India

Completion Date: 2010
Height to Architectural Top[1]: Tower A, C & D: 121m (397ft); Tower B: 134m (440ft)
Stories[1]: Tower A, C & D: 33; Tower B: 34
Area: 51,623 sq m (555,665 sq ft)
Primary Use[1]: Residential
Owner/Developer: Neo Pharma Pvt Ltd (A Kalpataru Group Co)
Design Architect: Ong & Ong Pte Ltd
Associate Architect: Goregaokar Architects
Structural Engineer: Pravin Gala & Associates
MEP Engineer: Techno Group

[1] For all definitions used in the data sections throughout this book, refer to CTBUH criteria shown on pages 184–187

Kwun Tong 223
Hong Kong, China

Completion Date: December 2009
Height to Architectural Top[1]: 105m (346ft)
Stories[1]: 22
Area: 101,493 sq m (1,092,461sq ft)
Primary Use[1]: Office
Owner: Profit System Development Ltd; Easewin Development Ltd & Morison Ltd
Developer: Henderson Land Development Co Ltd; Sun Hung Kai Properties Ltd
Design Architect: Dennis Lau & Ng Chun Man Architects and Engineers (HK) Ltd
Structural Engineer: Stephen Cheng Consulting Engineers Ltd
MEP Engineer: Parsons Brinckerhoff (Asia) Pte Ltd
Main Contractor: Heng Lai Construction Co Ltd

The Masterpiece
Hong Kong, China

Completion Date: February 2009
Height to Architectural Top[1]: 257m (843ft)
Stories[1]: 64
Area: 102,625 sq m (1,104,646 sq ft)
Primary Use[1]: Mixed: Residential/Hotel
Other Use: Retail
Owner/Developer: New World Development Co Ltd; Urban Renewal Authority
Design Architect: Dennis Lau & Ng Chun Man Architects and Engineers (HK) Ltd
Structural Engineer: Arup Hong Kong
MEP Engineer: Meinhardt (M&E) Ltd
Main Contractor: Hip Hing Builders Co Ltd
Other Consultants: Rider Levett Bucknall; OAP; Team 73 HK Ltd

The St. Francis Shangri-la Place
Mandaluyong City, Philippines

Completion Date: September 2009
Height to Architectural Top[1]: 213m (698ft)
Stories[1]: 60
Area: 107,473 sq m (1,156,830 sq ft)
Primary Use[1]: Residential
Owner/Developer: Shang Properties, Inc
Design Architect: Wong and Tung International Ltd
Associate Architect: Casas+Architects
Structural Engineer: Arup
MEP Engineer: WSP Hong Kong Ltd
Main Contractor: EEI Corporation
Other Consultants: Davis Langdon & Seah Ltd; Jose Aliling & Associates

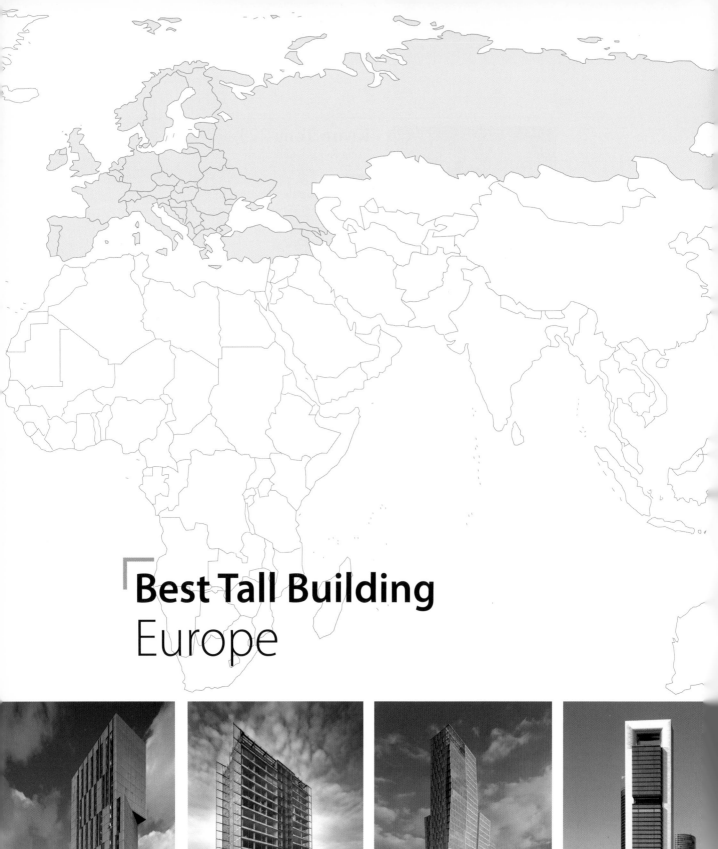

Best Tall Building
Europe

Broadcasting Place

Leeds, UK

Broadcasting Place is a mixed-use development close to Leeds city center. Conceived as a public/private partnership for property group Downing and Leeds Metropolitan University, it provides new office and teaching spaces together with 240 student residences. A new Baptist Church completes the scheme on its northern edge.

A bold addition to the Leeds cityscape, Broadcasting Place forms a prominent marker at one of Leeds' gateways. This new academic complex for Leeds Metropolitan University overcame difficult site challenges with a masterplan which manages an inner city motorway passing alongside while also enabling future growth. The site itself encompasses a rich history as the location of Old Broadcasting House, the old BBC TV Studios, and the place where the first moving picture was developed by Louis Le Prince in the late 19th century. It sets the ideal stage for an educational building dedicated to Leeds Met's Faculty of Arts and Society.

The masterplan worked within the framework of the "Renaissance Leeds" documents which defined a "city rim" where physical and social connectivity were paramount in reintegrating the city center with its inner city surroundings. The building concept attempts a fusion between the geological, the sculptural and the cinematic to create a building that is firmly rooted in its city context. The building creates two rising forms that snake around the perimeter of the site, responding to existing building heights, culminating in a tower "head" at the south side of the site. This tower marks the south end of the site with a dramatic formed gable end that faces towards the city.

Extensive negotiations were undertaken with the City Planning Department and in particular their Conservation Department. English Heritage was also involved in these discussions and after some initial opposition to the proposals ultimately wrote in support of the design.

This is a key central Leeds location and a new public space linking key urban spaces forms a significant landscape element in the scheme. Broadcasting Place opens up pedestrian routes across the site that had been blocked by previous developments and reconnects Woodhouse Lane with Blenheim Walk.

A key element in the design of the buildings is the irregular elevations which have been tailored to optimize daylight and reduce solar penetration. The proportions of the glazed façade have been derived using special software. An innovative analysis of the building façades was undertaken, to calculate the optimum quantity and distribution of glazing/shading

Completion Date: September 2009
Height to Architectural Top[1]: 70m (228ft)
Stories[1]: 23
Area: 6,486 sq m (69,815 sq ft)
Primary Use[1]: Mixed: Residential/Education/Office
Owner: Downing; Leeds Metropolitan University
Developer: Downing
Design Architect: Feilden Clegg Bradley Studios
Structural Engineer: Halcrow Yolles
MEP Engineer: KGA Trinity Chambers
Main Contractor: George Downing Construction
Other Consultants: Ridge and Partners; Robert Myers Associates; Matthew & Goodman; HE Simms

[1] For all definitions used in the data sections throughout this book, refer to CTBUH criteria shown on pages 184–187

Opposite: View from south of student housing tower

Left: Façade detail
Opposite Top: Atrium of academic building
Opposite Bottom: Tower entry viewed from central courtyard

> "The use of the cor-ten cladding responds to the natural materials of the groundscape while it's bold and confident steel form also resonates with the industrial engineering traditions of the city."
>
> *Peter Murray, Juror, New London Architecture Centre*

at all points on the façade in order to ensure high levels of natural day lighting but without overheating.

The buildings are conceived as solid landscape forms which draw on Yorkshire's rich geological and sculptural heritage. The concept of a strong roof pitch is reflected in the massing of the buildings which have sharp triangular corners and angular cantilevered projections. Through this massive form, windows were conceived as the flow of water cascading through a rock formation. This design intent is reinforced by the selection of cor-ten steel for the façade, as a solid, sculptural and weathering material.

The tower sits high above the city center on a main ridge which focuses a number of the city's taller buildings. The stepping mass of the tower front places the largest elements on the skyline and the smaller elements closer to the ground and human scale. This inversion of traditional stepped massing gives the tower a unique character that provides a new identity for Leeds Met University and Downing. The sculptural south elevation is free of windows reflecting the benefits of an east–west orientation for accommodation, while at the same time reinforcing the clarity of the sculpted form in the city.

Jury Statement

Broadcasting Place succeeds on many levels, addressing city and urban design, respect for surrounding heritage buildings, and a richness of architectural design. Its references to geological and sculptural context make the building intimately local, contemporary and beautiful at the same time. It creates a unique and interesting form on the Leeds skyline. The building has an iconic presence, but manages to remain unobtrusive and respectful of its locale, successfully knitting together a disparate piece of historic townscape with a new residential tower.

The design addresses sustainable design at the highest level, with concerns for day lighting and optimization of cooling loads and energy use being the prime drivers of form and the placement of glazing. The choice of cor-ten steel cladding brings a warmth to the tower as it unifies the composition of the complex and places contemporary and historic architecture into dynamic conversation.

The ascending scale of the grouped projections to the south is also reflected in the grouping of windows on the east and west elevations. Smaller shifts at the lower floors give the building a more intimate scale on the street, while larger groupings higher up are designed to be seen from long distances and deal with the city scale.

The environmental approach for the building combined several elements: the façade was designed to optimize cooling load and energy use through the rigorous research and development project involving 3D computer simulations of all façades, and the building's form was designed to optimize natural daylight and allow for natural ventilation where practicable. The development was also designed on the premise of being a car-free environment conducive to pedestrian access and includes a bike parking provision. During detailed design the buildings were developed to suit the Leeds Met University's specific needs for the various faculties, while not sacrificing future adaptability to ensure a long lifespan for the building.

Left: View of east elevation
Opposite Top: Office interior
Opposite Bottom: Typical housing floor plan

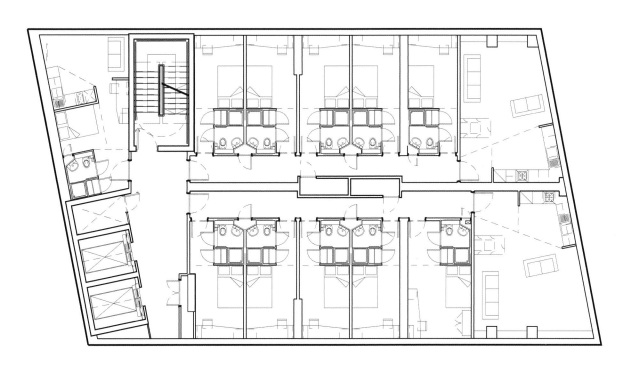

Hegau Tower

Singen, Germany

Simplicity of form and selective use of materials emphasizes the fundamental design idea behind the building—to formulate a clear statement of modernism. The building's components, structure and envelope, as well as the users and their activities within, are clearly legible through the transparent façades. The south west facing façade expands beyond the building volume vertically and horizontally. The screens form one continuous glass sheet along the forecourt, connecting both the low and high building components into one.

The tower is constructed as a concrete frame with stiffening core and perimeter columns. Structure and façade are designed for flexibility in office layouts and allow for an open plan or cellular offices as well as multiple tenants per floor. The raised floor provides the opportunity to revise electrical and data caballing systems as technology progresses. Lightweight partition systems allow fast and inexpensive adaptation of changing space requirements. The use of a single secured stair as escape route for the users improves an economy to the building with its relatively small floor plate.

Completion Date: 2009
Height to Architectural Top[1]**:** 68m (221ft)
Stories[1]**:** 18
Area: 17,056 sq m (183,589 sq ft)
Primary Use[1]**:** Office
Owner/Developer: GVV Singen
Design Architect: Murphy/Jahn Architects
Structural Engineer: Werner Sobek Ingenieure
MEP Engineer: Transsolar; IB Schwarz; Schreiber Ingenieure
Main Contractor: Züblin; FKN. GaTech

The interaction between all heating, ventilation and cooling components and their joint reaction to the exterior condition forms a complex and efficient system. Fan assisted heating and cooling convectors receive fresh air supply through the façade and bring in conditioned air directly without detour through centralized units. Heat recovery is achieved by running the return air through a heat exchanger, transferring its energy to the medium water for the thermal mass system.

Natural ventilation is provided by hopper windows operated by chain motors and held by scissor hinges. This allows the user to utilize fresh air for cooling, improvement of air quality and the experience of a connection to the outside.

The flat concrete slab is equipped with PVC water tubes to cool and heat the exposed thermal mass of the structure. The mass absorbs heat during the day and is cooled off actively and passively during the night. 30% of the basic cooling is thus covered without the need of energy and space consuming air convection.

The façade module of 2.7m (8.9ft) generates a generous ambiance of space. A windproof, exterior automatic operable sunshade on the south west façade allows for reduction of solar loads along with automatic interior perforated louvers on the other three façades. The exterior sunshade is a retractable curtain of stainless steel bars. Either by sensors or the user's command, the sunshade covers the entire façade reducing the solar load to a minimum while still providing a visual connection to the outside. The

Opposite: View from north

124

"This project is clearly all about the façade and the amazing transformations that take it from complete transparency to perforated opacity."

Antony Wood, Juror, CTBUH

shading screen is highly wind resistant and has had its first large scale application in the Hegau Tower project. While the façade is clearly a very strong element in the project, it does not just determine the visual appearance of the building, but importantly, it also forms the interface between its interior and the exterior in respect to thermal, acoustic and visual exchange. The basic design of the building's façade consists of large sheets of high-performance insulated glass with a transparent appearance yet effective sun-shading values. This basic and economic principal is amended by flexible components which allow the envelope to react to the requirements of the inner and conditions of the outer environment.

The façade becomes an integral part of the structure and technology of the building and a direct expression of the economical and ecological goals set forth in its design. The building's appearance consequently is in keeping with the urbanistic, aesthetic and technological relevance of the project for the city, region and the time of its inception.

Jury Statement

The simplicity of form and elegance of this all glass prism are pristinely executed. What sets this tower apart however, are the automatic sunshades on the south west façade. Either by sensor or user controls, the retractable metal screens animate the façade and bring a distinctive ever-changing character to the face of the building.

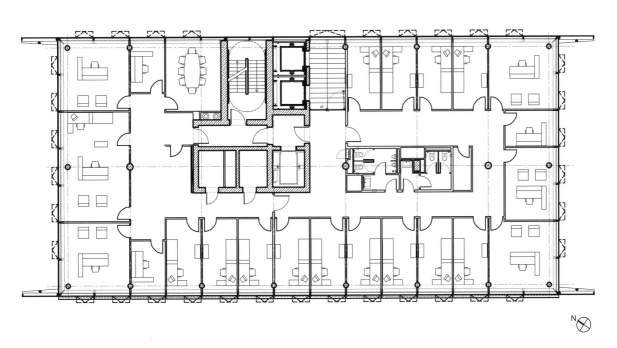

PalaisQuartier Office Tower
Frankfurt, Germany

Positioned outside the limits of the cluster of high-rises in the neighboring banking district, the PalaisQuartier forms the architectural highpoint of a new district in downtown Frankfurt—with shapes that catch the eye even from a great distance, its expressive shape creates an exciting counterpart. Together with the Thurn und Taxis Palais Townhouse (recently rebuilt to preserve its original façade), and the "MyZeil" shopping mall, the PalaisQuartier rounds out a new district which has a decidedly urban flair.

The urban planning concept from the outset envisaged the construction of an urban quarter on the former Post Office site that linked various facilities such as accommodation, hotels, offices, restaurants, event rooms and retail outlets with each other. The new combination of reconstructed space, inner-city shopping mall, office high-rise tower and hotel creates a lively urban place in the center of Frankfurt. The Thurn und Taxis Plaza forms the publicly accessible center of the new quarter, enriching the inner city.

Completion Date: April 2010
Height to Architectural Top[1]: 135m (443ft)
Stories[1]: 34
Area: 48,000 sq m (516,668 sq ft)
Primary Use[1]: Office
Owner/Developer: MAB Development Deutschland GmbH
Design Architect: KSP Juergen Engel Architekten GmbH
Structural Engineer: Weischede, Herrmann und Partner
MEP Engineer: Peter Berchtold Engineering Consultants
Main Contractor: BAM
Other Consultants: hhpberlin – Ingenieure für Brandschutz

Two materials, namely aluminum and glass, define the appearance of the face of the building, which is designed as segmented curtain façades. The eye-catching characteristic of the tower is, when seen from the side, the diamond-shaped fully glazed surfaces. They are integrated into the façade like crystalline bodies. In order to emphasize the crystalline character of the glass, diamonds are implemented as dual façades using highly transparent, untreated panes of glass as the outer layer, with solar protection integrated into the intervening space in the façade, and insulation-grade glass windows constituting the inner, thermal skin. If desired, the windows in the office high-rise can be opened to provide natural ventilation. The transparency of the high-rise façades with their non-reflecting windows makes it possible to look in and out, enlivening the high-rise and opening it up visually to its surroundings.

The tower's slightly tilted façades are structured by the three striking fold lines and their height, which is defined by the design and derived from the overall shape. Inspired by Constantin Brancusi's gleaming column-like artworks, the sculptural qualities of the office tower with its neighboring hotel tower serve as unmistakable points of orientation in the city's fabric.

The tapering/expansion that results from the tilting creates office footprints with different depths in line with the building's underlying geometry. The usable depth of the office areas, which are 3.05 m (10ft) high from floor-to-ceiling, is about 5.9m (19ft) in the tapered sections and up to 9.6m (31.5ft) in the zones that jut out furthest. This variance encourages a great

Opposite: View of office tower from north west (with Thurn und Taxis Palais in front)

"The zigzag frontage delivers a sculptural form without sacrificing the regular and efficient office spaces within."

Peter Murray, Juror, New London Architecture Centre

Left: Façade detail
Opposite Top: Aerial view in context
Opposite Bottom Left: Typical section
Opposite Bottom Right: Typical high zone floor plan (top) and low zone floor plan (bottom)

> **"The tilted façades reduce the bulk of the towers while adding a distinctive, recognizable quality to the development."**
>
> *Mun Summ Wong, Juror, WOHA Architects*

range of different office layouts, from executive offices via combined offices with a central area for communicative shared usage, through to open plan offices.

The energy concept envisages that about 50% of the heating/cooling energy requirement is covered by sus-

tainable systems. About 20% of the figure is obtained geothermally through a combined heat-pump and cooling system. The highly efficient central heat recovery plant relies on radiant heat from the shopping mall and the underground car park. It provides about 30% of the total heating energy requirement. The rented areas are cooled/heated by means of a heating control system for the respective building section integrated into the concrete ceilings. For this reason, there is no need for suspended ceilings in the sections containing office workstations. Ambient temperature, lighting and solar protection blinds are all centrally controlled by sensors, whereby they can be individually set at any time.

Jury Statement

The striking interrelationship of the tilted façades forms the central theme of the design of this office tower and its smaller neighboring hotel. The buildings are a major landmark in the new downtown area of this essentially low-rise city. The angular façades add a dynamic element to the form, whilst subtle variations in the fenestration help to further break up the façades. The towers emerge from the historic Thurn and Taxis townhouse creating a sharp contrast against the 18th century stone.

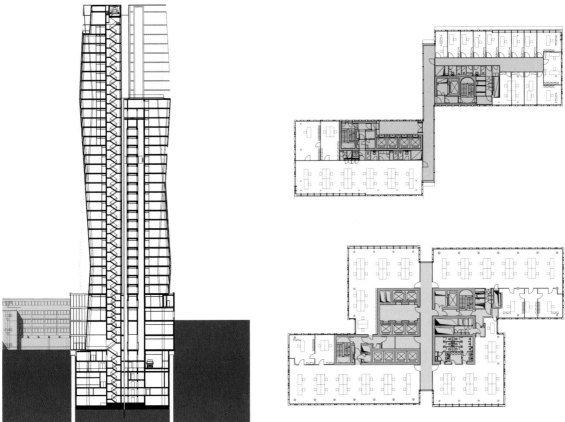

Caja Madrid Tower
Madrid, Spain

Compositionally the building can be thought of as a tall arch, the services and circulation cores framing open office floors. The orientation of the typical floor plan positions the unoccupied cores to the east and west to minimize heat gain on the inhabited space. The office space is enclosed within a unifying curtain wall system composed of triple glazed units with a solar protective coating and motorized internal blinds for glare control integrated within the cavity. The opening at the top of the building mitigates wind impact and is designed to house wind turbines as a possible future innovation.

Although the building is conceived as a corporate headquarters—housing Caja Madrid, the largest savings bank in Madrid—it also has the flexibility to be partly sub-let, enabling Caja Madrid to expand or contract its accommodation easily in the future as required. This degree of flexibility results in part from pushing the service cores to the edges of the plan to create uninterrupted 1,200 sq m (12,900 sq ft) floor plates. Vertical circulation routes occupy minimal space with the core area use being optimized through the installation of a lift destination control system.

Completion Date: 2009
Height to Architectural Top[1]: 248m (815ft)
Stories[1]: 45
Area: 77,500 sq m (834,203 sq ft)
Primary Use[1]: Office
Owner: Caja Madrid
Developer: Repsol YPF
Design Architect: Foster + Partners
Associate Architect: Gonzalo Martinez-Pita Copello; Javier Martin Minguez; Alatec
Structural Engineer: Halvorson and Partners; Arquing; Gilsanz Murray Steficek LLP
MEP Engineer: Aguilera Ingenieros S.A.
Main Contractor: FCC – ACS
Other Consultants: Emmer Pfenninger Partner AG

Top: Overall view
Bottom: Building lobby
Opposite Top Left: Ground floor plan
Opposite Bottom Left: Typical floor plan
Opposite Right: Typical section

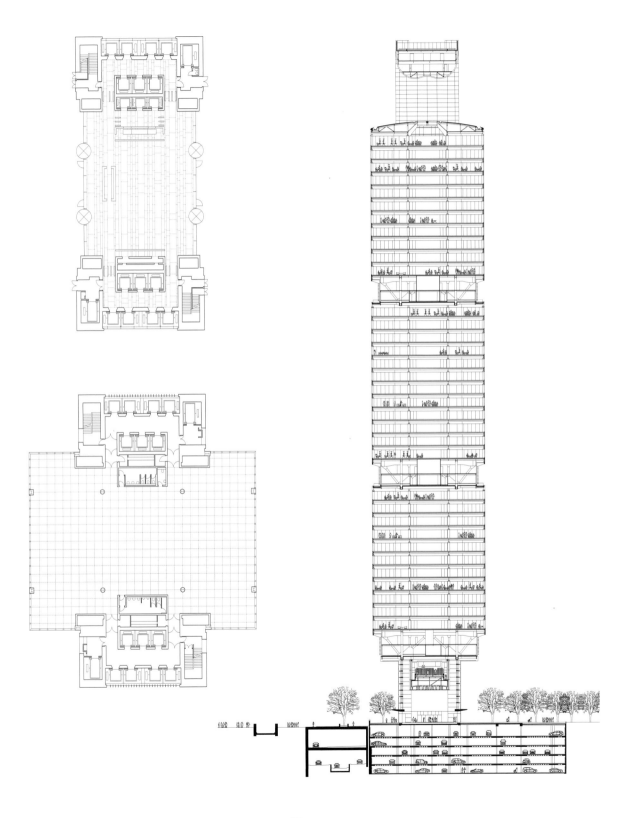

133

Mosfilmovskaya

Moscow, Russia

Mosfilmovskaya is composed of two towers which are unified by a third structure consisting of two parallel eight-story units, with a shared atrium that brings natural sunlight to the space. The complex is located near the open spaces of Poklonnaya Gora and the valley of the Setun River, and its composition is a reflection of this location. Positioned on a three-level base that contains underground parking lots, trade rooms, sport grounds, and separate office units, the connecting low story residences and main tower are lifted up 17m (56ft) by tilted columns made of cast-in-situ concrete.

The building's architecture responds to the scarceness of other large buildings in the district, and the famous rich greenery of the Moscow State University campus and vast territories of the well-known "Mosfilm" factory of movies. A principle of segregation between private and public spaces was part of the fundamental program for the complex. Separation from residential users, office users and visitors, while concurrently providing all users access to the buildings' many functions, was realized through optimization and planning to avoid loss of engineering and technology efficiency.

Completion Date: 2010
Height to Architectural Top[1]: 213m (700ft)
Stories[1]: 53
Area: 220,715 sq m (2,375,756 sq ft)
Primary Use[1]: Residential
Other Use: Office, Retail
Owner: DONSTROY Corporation
Developer: DS Development
Design Architect: Architectural Bureau of Sergey Skuratov
Structural Engineer: I. Shipetin Design Bureau
MEP Engineer: Alexej Kolubkov
Main Contractor: DONSTROY Corporation

Top: Overall view
Bottom: Façade detail
Opposite Left: View of eight-story atrium from ground level
Opposite Right: Typical floor plans

The construction site was chosen precisely at the break point of the longitudinal profile on the famous Mosfilmovskaya Street, and occupied only vacant spaces within the city block. To stress the size of the main tower, an eight-shade aluminum panel system from Japan was used as the finishing element to the suspended façade. These panels create a smooth transition from a bright white Carrara marble look at the top, to a dark shade of limestone at the bottom. A rhombus shaped floor plan is slightly but intentionally turned counterclockwise as it travels upwards, thus giving the main tower a slightly twisted shape. Its façades are made of three different types of glass, while the intertwining, basket-weave stripes subdue its monotony. Multiple outlets for retail and entertainment are seen throughout the building's program, including a self-service store below the building's ground level as well as shopping galleries, and a night club.

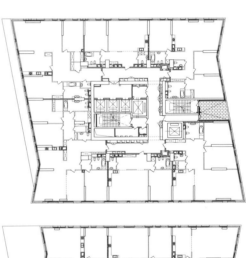

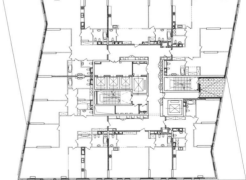

Stadthaus

London, UK

Stadthaus is thought to be amongst the tallest timber residential structures in the world. It is the first high-density housing building to be built from pre-fabricated cross-laminated timber panels (using spruce planks glued together with a non-toxic adhesive), including all load-bearing walls and floor slabs as well as stair and lift cores. Each panel is prefabricated including cutouts for windows and doors and routed service channels. As the panels arrived on site they were immediately craned into position and fixed in place. Four carpenters assembled the nine-story structure in 27 days. The speed of the construction in such a densely populated environment is especially relevant, as was the lack of noise and waste, creating far less intrusion on the local community.

Concerns associated with timber buildings are predominantly related to acoustics and fire protection. Timber buildings are classified as poor in terms of their acoustic performance due to the light structure as compared to reinforced concrete and masonry. However, cross-laminated solid timber panels have a significantly higher density than timber frame buildings. They provide a solid structural core on

Completion Date: January 2009
Height to Architectural Top[1]: 29m (95ft)
Stories[1]: 9
Area: 2,890 sq m (31,108 sq ft)
Primary Use[1]: Residential
Owner: Telford Homes; Metropolitan Housing Trust
Developer: Telford Homes
Design Architect: Waugh Thistleton Architects
Structural Engineer: Techniker Ltd
MEP Engineer: Michael Popper and Associates; AJD Design Partnership
Main Contractor: Telford Homes
Other Consultants: KLH, UK

Top: Overall view
Bottom: Interior construction
Opposite Top Left: Typical social housing floor plan
Opposite Bottom Left: Construction detail section at exterior wall
Opposite Top Right: Interior construction view
Opposite Bottom Right: Interior finished view

which different, independent and separating layers can be added. In Stadthaus an economic layering strategy of stud walls, floating floor build-ups and suspended ceilings, gave sound attenuation far in excess of building regulations (58–60db).

In a fire, solid timber elements, such as cross-laminated timber panels, take longer to burn than dimensional lumber. For Stadthaus a series of tests were conducted allowing the design team to demonstrate a fire resistance of 90 minutes. This is based on the charring rates of the timber panel and two layers of plasterboard. The actual performance would be even better, since the calculations are conservative and do not take into account timber's ability to "self protect" once a layer of char forms on its surface.

It was a requirement from the social housing client that a separate ground floor entrance was provided for the affordable units. This resulted in a mirrored floor plan from east to west, with an identical entrance to each aspect. Both tenures are served by an individual staircase and lift. The five upper stories are designated for private sale and the three lower for social housing.

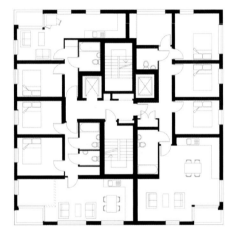

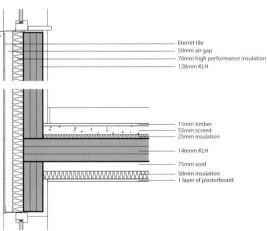

Eternit tile
50mm air gap
70mm high performance insulation
128mm KLH

15mm timber
55mm screed
25mm insulation
146mm KLH
75mm void
50mm insulation
1 layer of plasterboard

Strata SE1
London, UK

Strata SE1 constitutes a key element in the Elephant & Castle Regeneration Masterplan. This 408-apartment development has a modest footprint which creates additional areas of public realm at ground level. The scheme also includes an adjacent five-story pavilion building that will comprise residential and retail facilities. Strata will be connected to the planned Elephant & Castle MUSCo (Multi-Utility Services Company), a community combined heating and power scheme which uses renewable resources.

The tower has in many ways been shaped by both short and long-distance views of its form; hence the articulation and grain of its distinctive cladding are designed to both make their mark on the London skyline as well as creating a strong sense of human scale that engages the public when viewed close-up.

The first building in the world with cladding-enclosed wind turbines, it sets a new benchmark in terms of environmental strategy. The use of integrated wind turbines is a visually exciting means of generating electricity for a building of this height and location.

Completion Date: July 2010
Height to Architectural Top[1]: 148m (485ft)
Stories[1]: 43
Area: 35,715 sq m (384,431 sq ft)
Primary Use[1]: Residential
Owner: Castle House Developments Ltd
Developer: Brookfield Developments UK Ltd
Design Architect: BFLS
Structural Engineer: WSP Group
MEP Engineer: WSP Group
Main Contractor: Brookfield Constructions UK Ltd
Other Consultants: URS Corporation Ltd; RWDI, Inc; Norwin AS

Top: Overall view from the south east
Bottom: Detail view of wind turbine
Opposite: From left to right: west, south, and north elevations

The form and orientation of the building enables the best use of the dominant prevailing south–south west wind direction. The three five-bladed, 9m (30ft) diameter wind turbines are rated at 19kW each and are anticipated to produce 50Mwh of electricity per year, approximately 8% of the building's estimated total energy consumption. To put this figure into context, it is enough energy to meet the total annual demand from 30 two-bedroom apartments (based on current 2006 Building Regulations). The electricity generated by the turbines will be used to supplement the landlords' supply for the common areas of the building. The actual energy output of the wind turbines will be published after two years of comprehensive wind data analysis.

Each layer of the façade has been tuned to vary its performance where appropriate. Glass, the most precious and vulnerable layer, is located on the inside, with a solid aluminum panel forming the outermost layer and an intermediate zone that contains the ventilation zones and opening panels. The solid operable vents on the building's façade allow for natural ventilation.

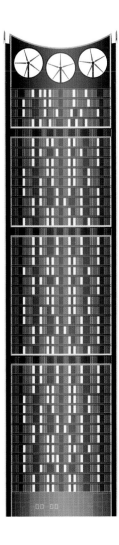
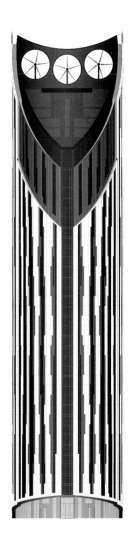

Candle House
Leeds, UK

Completion Date: February 2010
Height to Architectural Top[1]**:** 73m (240ft)
Stories[1]**:** 22
Area: 12,385 sq m (133,311 sq ft)
Primary Use[1]**:** Residential
Owner/Developer: ISIS Waterside Regeneration
Design Architect: CareyJones Architects
Structural Engineer: Ramboll
MEP Engineer: Buro Happold
Main Contractor: Ardmore
Other Consultants: Davis Langdon & Seah Ltd; Lovejoy

Imperia Tower
Moscow, Russia

Completion Date: September 2010
Height to Architectural Top[1]**:** 239m (783ft)
Stories[1]**:** 60
Area: 281,236 sq m (3,027,199 sq ft)
Primary Use[1]**:** Mixed: Residential/Hotel/Office
Owner: ZAO "Fleiner-City"
Developer: GDO GROUP
Design Architect: NBBJ
Main Contractor: Enka Insaat ve Sanayi A.S.

Maastoren
Rotterdam, The Netherlands

Completion Date: December 2009
Height to Architectural Top[1]**:** 165m (541ft)
Stories[1]**:** 44
Area: 69,000 sq m (742,710 sq ft)
Primary Use[1]**:** Office
Owner: SEB Investment GmbH
Developer: OVG projectontwikkeling BV
Design Architect: Dam & Partners Architecten
Structural Engineer: Ingenieursbureau Zonneveld BV
MEP Engineer: Techniplan Adviseurs BV
Main Contractor: Besix Group

[1] For all definitions used in the data sections throughout this book, refer to CTBUH criteria shown on pages 184–187

The Mill and Jerwood Dance House
Ipswich, UK

Completion Date: October 2009
Height to Architectural Top[1]: 71m (233ft)
Stories[1]: 23
Area: 4,500 sq m (48,438 sq ft)
Primary Use[1]: Residential
Other Use: Dance Studio
Owner: Wharfside Properties
Design Architect: John Lyall Architects
Structural Engineer: Walsh Associates; Price and Myers
MEP Engineer: Harley Hadow; Emcor Limited
Main Contractor: Laing O'Rourke; Morgan Ashurst

Opernturm
Frankfurt, Germany

Completion Date: December 2009
Height to Architectural Top[1]: 170m (558ft)
Stories[1]: 42
Area: 74,489 sq m (801,792 sq ft)
Primary Use[1]: Office
Other Use: Retail
Owner: Opernplatz Property Holdings GmbH & Co KG
Developer: Tishman Speyer Property
Design Architect: Prof. Mäckler Architekten
Associate Architect: MOW Generalplanung
Structural Engineer: BGS; Bollinger Grohmann
MEP Engineer: Techdesign; Ebener & Partner
Main Contractor: Züblin

Sea Towers
Gdynia, Poland

Completion Date: August 2009
Height to Architectural Top[1]: 127m (418ft)
Stories[1]: 37
Area: 54,968 sq m (591,671 sq ft)
Primary Use[1]: Residential
Owner/Developer: Invest Komfort SA
Design Architect: Architekturbüro Andrzej Kapuscik
Structural Engineer: BWL Projekt Sp.zo.o.
MEP Engineer: Klimaster Sp.zo.o.; Record Sp.zo.o.; Mercury Engineering Polska Sp.zo.o.
Main Contractor: Modzelewski + Rodek Sp.zo.o.
Other Consultants: Vis a Vis Design Studio; RS-AK

Best Tall Building
Middle East & Africa

Burj Khalifa

Dubai, UAE

Burj Khalifa has redefined what is possible in the design and engineering of supertall buildings. By combining cutting-edge technologies and cultural influences, the building serves as a global icon that is both a model for future urban centers and speaks to the global movement towards compact, livable urban areas. The Tower and its surrounding neighborhood are more centralized than any other new development in Dubai. At the center of a new downtown neighborhood, Burj Khalifa's mixed-use program focuses the area's development density and provides direct connections to mass transit systems.

Burj Khalifa's architecture has embodied references to Islamic architecture and yet reflects the modern global community it is designed to serve. The building's Y-shaped plan provides the maximum amount of perimeter for windows in living spaces without developing internal unusable area. As the tapering tower rises, setbacks occur at the ends of each "wing" in an upward spiraling pattern that decreases the mass of the tower as the height increases. These setbacks were modeled in the wind tunnel to minimize wind forces. The design of the Tower was significantly influenced by its performance with respect to the wind, in both its shaping and orientation. The building went through many wind tunnel tests and design iterations to develop optimum performance.

The exterior cladding, comprised of aluminum and textured stainless steel spandrel panels, was designed to withstand Dubai's extreme temperatures during the summer months by using a low-E glass to provide enhanced thermal insulation. Vertical polished stainless steel fins were added to accentuate Burj Khalifa's height and slenderness.

The unprecedented height of the Burj Khalifa required it to be an innovative building in many ways. Design techniques, building systems, and construction practices all required rethinking, and in many cases new applications, to create a practical and efficient building.

The structural system, termed a "buttressed core," is designed to efficiently support a supertall building utilizing a strong central core, buttressed by its three wings. The vertical structure is tied together at the mechanical floors through outrigger walls in order to maximize the building's stiffness. The result is an efficient system where all of the building's vertical structure is used to support both gravity and lateral loads.

The Tower incorporates numerous enhancements to the fire and life safety systems, including "lifeboat" operation for elevators which allows for them to be

Completion Date: January 2010
Height to Architectural Top[1]**:** 828m (2,717ft)
Stories[1]**:** 163
Area: 302,586 sq m (3,257,009 sq ft)
Primary Use[1]**:** Mixed: Office/Residential/Hotel
Owner/Developer: Emaar Properties PJSC
Design Architect: Skidmore, Owings & Merrill LLP
Associate Architect: Hyder Consulting
Structural Engineer: Skidmore, Owings & Merrill LLP
MEP Engineer: Skidmore, Owings & Merrill LLP
Main Contractor: Samsung; Besix Group; Arabtec
Other Consultants: Turner International; Lerch Bates & Associates; RWDI, Inc; The Boundary Layer Wind Tunnel Laboratory; STS Consultants; The RJA Group, Inc; SWA Group

[1] For all definitions used in the data sections throughout this book, refer to CTBUH criteria shown on pages 184–187

Opposite: Context view within Downtown Dubai area with The Old Town in the foreground and Skeikh Zayed Road in the background.

"This project has redefined a region and a people, created a sense of place for Dubai, advanced the technologies of supertall buildings and established a new benchmark for the integrated practice of architecture and engineering."

Gordon Gill, Awards Chair, Adrian Smith + Gordon Gill Architecture

"Towering over Dubai's skyline, the design creates a global icon for 21st century architecture and engineering that will be studied for years to come."

Bruce Kuwabara, Juror, KPMB Architects

used for controlled evacuation under certain situations, decreasing total evacuation time by 45% over stairs alone.

Due to its height, the building is able to utilize ventilation where cooler air temperatures, reduced air density, and reduced relative humidity at the top of the building allow for "sky-sourced" fresh air. When air is drawn in at the top of the building, it requires less energy for air conditioning, ventilation, and dehumidification. The building's height also generates a substantial stack effect due to the thermal differences between the buildings' interior and exterior, but Burj Khalifa was designed to passively control these forces, reducing the need for mechanical means of pressurization.

Burj Khalifa has one of the largest condensate recovery systems in the world. Collecting water from air conditioning condensate discharge prevents it from entering the wastewater stream and reduces the need for municipal potable water.

The tower's management systems utilize smart lighting and mechanical controls which lower operational costs, allow for a more efficient use of building resources and services and better control of internal comfort conditions. Individual electric energy monitoring systems enable energy optimization of the tower's systems over its lifetime.

With over 185,800 sq m (2,000,000 sq ft) of interior space designed for Burj Khalifa, planning of the

Jury Statement

Undoubtedly one of the wonders of the modern world, Burj Khalifa is graceful and elegant as it reaches upward with seeming ease. The building's iconic status reflects the aspirations of Dubai to establish itself among the world's great cities. Through its ambition, style, and record-breaking height, it has instantly become one of the most recognizable buildings of our time.

The execution of this project was unprecedented in scale. Burj Khalifa utilized the latest technological advances in design, construction, and materials. It pushed the limits on the entire design and construction processes of high-rise buildings to a new level, emerging as a catalyst for a new surge of tall building systems and concepts all around the world. Carefully crafted around the wind forces, the Y-shaped plan and attenuated, stepped massing that bring the building to its pinnacle are at once beautiful and efficient.

building's interior space began at the earliest stages of its design focusing on three main goals—to recognize and acknowledge the building's height, to integrate its structural and architectural rationale, and to appreciate the locale's heritage, history and culture. The interiors of the uppermost floors were designed to reflect celestial influences. This is in contrast to the lower floors, which are inspired by natural elements.

An art program for the Tower was developed in which over 500 individual pieces of art were placed and specified throughout the Tower. The premier featured art piece resides in the tower's residential lobby. This sculpture, completed by the internationally renowned artist Jaume Plensa, is entitled "World Voices" and is composed of 196 cymbals supported by stainless steel rods rising from two pools similar to reeds in a lake. The cymbals represent the 196 countries of the world and reflect that the Burj Khalifa was a result of a collaboration of many people from around the world.

Left: Night view from the south east with the Dubai Fountain in foreground
Opposite Left: Elevation
Opposite Right: From top to bottom: typical office, typical residential and typical hotel floor plans

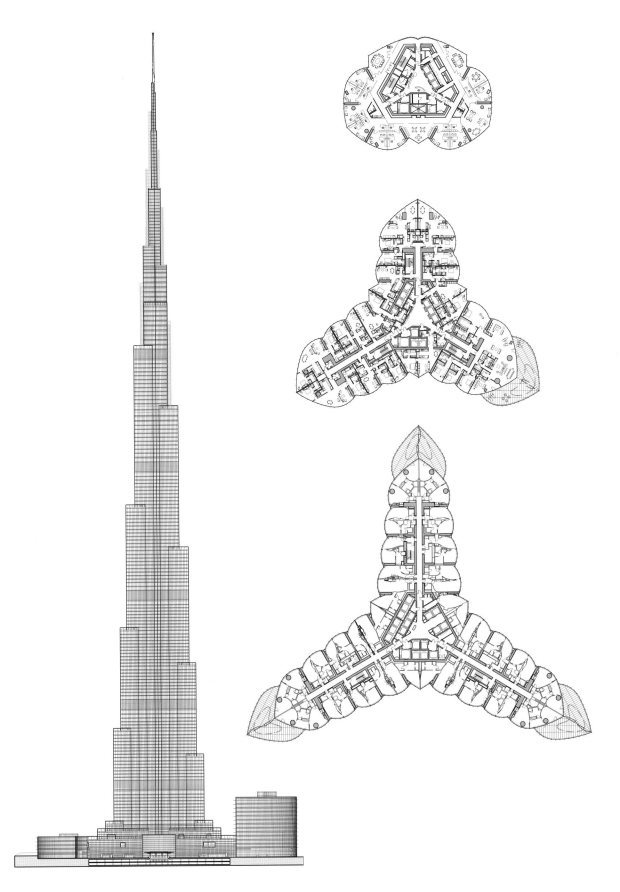

149

O-14
Dubai, UAE

The concrete shell of O-14 provides an efficient structural exoskeleton that frees the core from the burden of lateral forces and creates highly efficient, column-free open spaces in the building's interior. The exoskeleton of O-14 becomes the primary vertical and lateral structure for the building, allowing the column-free office slabs to span between it and the minimal core. By moving the lateral bracing for the building to the perimeter, the core, which is traditionally enlarged to receive lateral loading in most curtain wall office towers, can be minimized for only vertical loading, utilities, and transportation. Additionally, the typical curtain wall tower configuration results in floor plates that must be thickened to carry lateral loads to the core, yet in O-14 these can be minimized to only respond to span and vibration.

O-14 attempts to create a better urban condition as best it can within its limited site. Rather than assuming that the podium base would simply have an active front, O-14 subsumes the typical arcade into its shell, and produces another layer of activity higher up on the podium top. The parking is moved to four underground levels and the normally ground-level podium is elevated, thus freeing up the ground plane, and a continuous elevated pedestrian level—a "new ground"—is created above the street level. The promise is that O-14 and its neighbors could produce activity on many levels, and engender new kinds of connections from the rear street to the promenade, activating the waterfront block as a kind of infrastructure for the district.

O-14 is sheathed in a 40cm (15.7in) thick concrete shell perforated by over 1,300 openings that create a lace-like effect on the building's façade. The shell is organized as a diagrid, the efficiency of which is wed to a system of continuous variation of openings, always maintaining a minimum structural member, adding material locally where necessary and taking away where possible. This efficiency and modulation enables the shell to create a wide range of atmospheric and visual effects in the structure without changing the basic structural form, allowing for systematic analysis and construction. As a result, the pattern design is a combination of a capillary branching field, gradients of vertical articulation, opacity, environmental effects, a structural field, and a turbulence field.

In order to create the perforated exoskeleton, O-14 uses a slip-form construction technique: modular steel concrete forms are used then moved along the building axis, preventing costly dismantling and setup of complex shapes. The holes are achieved by weaving Computer Numerically Cut (CNC) polystyrene void forms into the reinforcement matrix of the shell, around which are constructed the slip forms of the interior and exterior surfaces of the shell. Super-liquid

Completion Date: June 2010
Height to Architectural Top[1]**:** 106m (347ft)
Stories[1]**:** 24
Area: 16,073 sq m (173,005 sq ft)
Primary Use[1]**:** Office
Owner/Developer: Creekside Development Corporation
Design Architect: Reiser + Umemoto, RUR Architecture, PC
Associate Architect: ERGA Progress
Structural Engineer: Ysrael A. Seinuk, PC
MEP Engineer: ERGA Progress
Main Contractor: Dubai Contracting Company LLC
Other Consultants: R.A. Heintges & Associates

Opposite: Overall view looking up

"The curvaceous, porous form creates a sculptural shell that is monumental and ambiguous on the exterior and intimate and sheltered on the interior."

Bruce Kuwabara, Juror, KPMB Architects

Left: Typical interior office space
Opposite Left Top: Typical floor plan
Opposite Left Bottom: West elevation
Opposite Right: Bridges connect building podium to main tower

> "The façade expression is simultaneously fun and serious, creating dynamic internal light intensities, as well as framed views out."

Antony Wood, Juror, CTBUH

concrete is then cast around this fine meshwork of reinforcement and void forms, resulting in the perforated exterior shell. Once the concrete has cured, the forms are loosened and moved up the tower to the next level, where the process begins again.

Jury Statement

O-14's façade is an innovative fusion of structure and exterior solar shading that is based on a perforated exoskeleton that dissolves the conventional reading of the building as an "office tower." The varying openings in the shell create a dazzling show of natural light, which creates a unique and ever changing sense of interior space. It is a welcomed departure from the standard glass-clad box; a fitting solution given its desert environment.

The shell acts not only as the primary structure of the building but also as a sunscreen open to light, air, and views. The openings on the shell thus modulate according to structural requirements, views, sun exposure, and luminosity. The overall pattern is not in response to a fixed program; rather the pattern in its modulation of solid and void will affect the arrangement of whatever program comes to occupy the floor plates. A 1m (3ft) gap between the main enclosure and exterior shell creates a so-called "chimney effect," a phenomenon whereby hot air has room to rise and effectively cools the surface of the glass windows behind the perforated shell. This passive solar technique is a natural component of the cooling system for O-14, reducing energy consumption and costs by more than 30%.

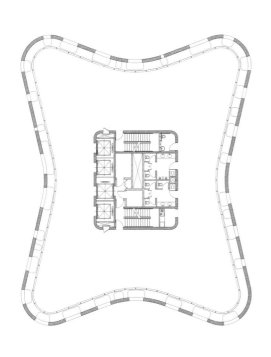

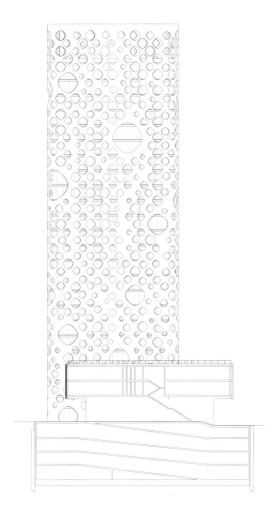

Al Bidda Tower

Doha, Qatar

Located at a prominent location in the heart of the Dafna Area overlooking the corniche, Al Bidda Tower's dramatic twisting face makes it unique amongst the other towers of the Doha skyline. The rounded triangular shaped floor plan of the tower has been conceptualized such that it is larger in floor area at the top floor than at its base, giving an elegant profile. This is enhanced by the cut roof shape under which there is a five-story open atrium. The tower is clad in an unconventional diagonal curtain wall that accommodates the progressively enlarging floor plate, as well as the shift of 60 degrees at the apex of the rounded triangular shaped roof.

The resulting multi-faced glass reflects the sunlight and nearby water during the day and artificial interior light during the night in various directions, giving the façade a jewel like luster. Every floor is unique, both in plate size and geometric location. In order to maximize rentable floor area there are no internal columns. The external columns twist with the building, and thus slope in two directions. To resist the resulting lateral loads, a braced steel diagrid is utilized, reflecting the triangular curtain wall system.

Completion Date: September 2009
Height to Architectural Top[1]: 197m (645ft)
Stories[1]: 43
Area: 55,552 sq m (597,956 sq ft)
Primary Use[1]: Office
Owner/Developer: Platinum Tower Co
Design Architect: GHD Global Pty Ltd
Structural Engineer: GHD Global Pty Ltd
MEP Engineer: GHD Global Pty Ltd
Main Contractor: Higgs & Hill/Qatari Arabian Construction Company JV
Other Consultants: Hill International

Top: Overall view in context
Bottom: Rendering of building atrium interior
Opposite Left: Typical floor plan
Opposite Right: Building elevations

In order to reduce the effects of increased loading to the steel bracing in the diagrid, the installation of the bracing into the external frame was delayed by 56 days after concrete casting. During this period it was estimated that approximately 45% of the total expected creep and axial shortening would have occurred, thereby reducing the expected increase in loading to the diagrid steel bracing.

Being located in Doha where temperatures and solar gain in summer can be high, and being totally clad in a glass curtain wall, posed some challenges in terms of ensuring occupant comfort and air conditioning efficiencies. The thermal performance of the façade had a significant impact on building energy consumption. The thermal performance of the framing system also had a considerable effect on the overall performance of the façade, and the combined thermal effects of the frame and glazing were accurately calculated to determine the total thermal performance of the system. Double glazing incorporating low-E glass was adopted following extensive testing. The façade work was made more complicated by the building geometry, where every triangular panel is different.

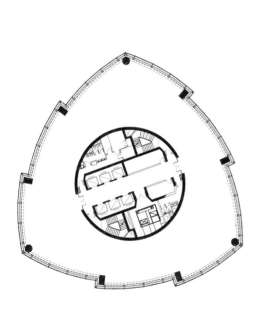

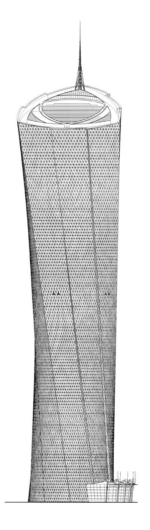

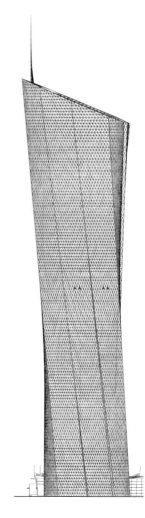

Al Tijaria Tower
Kuwait City, Kuwait

The form of Al Tijaria Tower (also known as the Kuwait Trade Center) is inspired by a spiral or helix. The body of the tower "twists" by 80 degrees as it climbs from the ground level to the top-most occupied floor. The tower plate is organized with a circular-shaped core located in the center of the floor. A concentric ring of structural columns allows for variation in slab edge location while keeping columns vertically aligned from floor to floor. This slab edge adjustment creates a twisted exterior massing for the tower. The tower features internal, vertically stacked, six-story-high atrium gardens rising through the height of the tower. The stacked atrium gardens spin around the center of the plate, creating a dynamic twisted space rising through the tower.

The exterior cladding design of the tower is a smooth aluminum and glass unitized curtain wall system. Materials include insulated blue-tinted vision and spandrel glass with selected use of silver aluminum panels. Glazing the atrium is insulated "clear" low-E glass (with custom ceramic frit pattern to control solar heat gain) supported by a stainless steel point-fixation system. Contrasting the tower, the podium is clad in a

Completion Date: September 2009
Height to Architectural Top[1]: 218m (716ft)
Stories[1]: 41
Area: 24,500 sq m (263,716 sq ft)
Primary Use[1]: Office
Other Use: Retail
Owner/Developer: Commercial Real Estate Company
Design Architect: Al-Jazera Consultants
Associate Architect: NORR Group
Structural Engineer: Al-Jazera Consultants
MEP Engineer: Al-Jazera Consultants
Main Contractor: SHBC Contracting Company
Other Consultants: Kevan Shaw

Top: Overall view from south west
Bottom: View of one of the six-story atriums
Opposite Left: Typical floor plan
Opposite Right: South elevation

combination of natural stone and pre-cast concrete. The Tower is composed of a five-story podium shopping mall, with an open-to-sky garden terrace on the podium roof, and an office tower rising above. The structural system of the shopping mall is a waffle slab with columns located on a 9m x 9m (29.5ft x 29.5ft) grid. Office floors are reinforced concrete slabs supported on structural steel beams. The floor plates rotate 20 degrees clockwise as they rise. Horizontal stability was provided using a number of strong core walls together with a 21m (69ft) diameter core wall in the tower area. The twelve equally-spaced tower columns are reinforced concrete, or composite with steel built up sections.

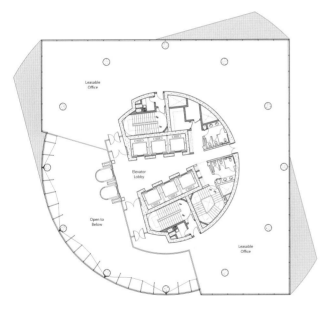

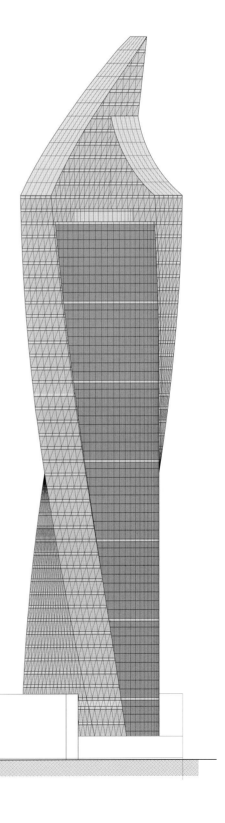

Arraya Office Tower
Kuwait City, Kuwait

A rraya Tower reaches new heights for Kuwait, as the first project to rise above Kuwait City's skyline after a height restriction was lifted. An impetus for revialization of an older rundown residential neighborhood, the Tower joined the Arraya Commerical Complex to become a seed project for the siginificant development of Kuwait City's new "downtown" business district.

The design sites the building's orientation with a north-facing glass curtain wall façade, while a concrete sheer wall faces west to deflect solar heat gain on the most susceptible side. The limestone-colored metal cladding reflects the harsh sun. The north facing façade, which is embraced by a community plaza and serves as a pedestrian entrance, floods the space with natural daylight while offering magnificent views to the Kuwait Gulf. The high-performing glass has a low-E, spectrally selective coating with a high shading coefficient that enhances the building's energy efficiency. The Commercial Complex's master plan also sites Arraya Tower with optimal pedestrian access in relationship to the hotel, retail complex and parking garage.

Completion Date: April 2009
Height to Architectural Top[1]: 300m (984ft)
Stories[1]: 60
Area: 59,292 sq m (638,213 sq ft)
Primary Use[1]: Office
Owner/Developer: Salhia Real Estate Company
Design Architect: Fentress Architects
Associate Architect: Pan Arab Consulting Engineers
Structural Engineer: Pan Arab Consulting Engineers
MEP Engineer: Pan Arab Consulting Engineers
Main Contractor: Ahmadiah Contracting and Trading Company

Top: Aerial view at dusk
Bottom: Building entry

Above: Overall view

Ocean Heights
Dubai, UAE

Ocean Heights is located in the Dubai Marina development, making an immediate visual impact through a combination of soaring height and the geometry of its form. The building immediately starts to twist its three faces at the base. As it rises, the tower's floor plates reduce in size, allowing the rotation to become even more pronounced. At 50 stories, the building rises over its neighbors. This movement allows two faces of the building unobstructed views of the ocean. The tower breaks away from the orthogonal grid and reorients the project toward one of Dubai's Palm Islands to the north.

A challenging aspect of the design was accommodating the client's strict requirement of unit layouts within a challenging envelope. What resulted was a rational 4m (13ft) module, which tracks its way down through the entire building and only changes at the façade. This also considerably simplified the structural system of the project. The shear walls were placed perpendicular to the mean of the two most extreme angles of the façade. This was done to soften the relationship between façade and partitions minimizing how "off-perpendicular" the relationship becomes.

Completion Date: August 2010
Height to Architectural Top[1]: 310m (1,017ft)
Stories[1]: 83
Area: 113,416 sq m (1,220,800 sq ft)
Primary Use[1]: Residential
Owner/Developer: Damac Gulf Properties LLC
Design Architect: Aedas Ltd
Associate Architect: ECG Engineering Consultants Group
Structural Engineer: Meinhardt Ltd
MEP Engineer: Ian Banham & Associates Consulting Engineers
Main Contractor: Arabtec

The Address
Dubai, UAE

Completion Date: October 2009
Height to Architectural Top[1]**:** 302m (991ft)
Stories[1]**:** 63
Area: 178,000 sq m (1,915,976 sq ft)
Primary Use[1]**:** Mixed: Residential/Hotel
Owner: Emaar Properties PJSC
Design Architect: Atkins
Structural Engineer: Atkins
MEP Engineer: Atkins
Main Contractor: Besix/Arabtec JV

Al Salam Tecom Tower
Dubai, UAE

Completion Date: May 2009
Height to Architectural Top[1]**:** 195m (640ft)
Stories[1]**:** 47
Area: 94,500 sq m (1,017,189 sq ft)
Primary Use[1]**:** Mixed: Residential/Office
Owner/Developer: Abdulsalam Alrafi Group
Design Architect: Atkins
Structural Engineer: Atkins
MEP Engineer: Atkins
Main Contractor: Belhasa Engineering & Contracting Co

Boulevard Plaza
Dubai, UAE

Completion Date: August 2010
Height to Architectural Top[1]**:** 168m (553ft)
Stories[1]**:** 37
Area: 101,425 sq m (1,091,730 sq ft)
Primary Use[1]**:** Office
Owner/Developer: Emaar Properties PJSC
Design Architect: Aedas Ltd
Structural Engineer: Hyder Consulting
MEP Engineer: Hyder Consulting
Main Contractor: Samsung/Baytur JV
Other Consultants: ALT Cladding; Schirmer Engineering

[1] For all definitions used in the data sections throughout this book, refer to CTBUH criteria shown on pages 184–187

Nassima Tower
Dubai, UAE

Completion Date: January 2010
Height to Architectural Top[1]: 204m (669ft)
Stories[1]: 49
Area: 221,113 sq m (2,380,041 sq ft)
Primary Use[1]: Mixed: Residential/Office
Developer: M.ACICO Real Estate Agent LLC
Design Architect: BRT Architekten
Structural Engineer: Dimensions Engineering Consultants
MEP Engineer: Hastie International
Main Contractor: ACICO Construction

Sama Tower
Dubai, UAE

Completion Date: May 2010
Height to Architectural Top[1]: 194m (635ft)
Stories[1]: 51
Area: 93,950 sq m (1,011,269 sq ft)
Primary Use[1]: Mixed: Residential/Office
Owner: Al Hamid Group
Design Architect: Atkins
Structural Engineer: Atkins
MEP Engineer: Atkins
Main Contractor: Dubai Contracting Company LLC

Tiffany Tower
Dubai, UAE

Completion Date: September 2009
Height to Architectural Top[1]: 182m (597ft)
Stories[1]: 45
Area: 49,000 sq m (527,431 sq ft)
Primary Use[1]: Office
Owner: IFFCO
Design Architect: Atkins
Structural Engineer: Atkins
MEP Engineer: Atkins
Main Contractor: M/S Al Rostamani Pegel

Lifetime Achievement
Awards Criteria

Lynn S. Beedle Award

The award recognizes an individual who has made extraordinary contributions to the advancement of tall buildings and the urban environment during his or her professional career. These contributions and leadership are recognized by the professional community and have significant effects, which extend beyond the professional community, to enhance cities and the lives of their inhabitants. The individual's contributions may be well known or little known by the public and may take any form, such as completed projects, research, technology, methods, ideas, or industry leadership.

The candidate may be from any area of specialization, including, but not limited to: architecture, structure, building systems, construction, academia, planning, development or management. The award emphasizes the unique, multi-disciplinary nature of the Council and is thus set apart from other professional organizations' awards for single disciplines.

In the case of both Lifetime Achievement Awards, the candidate may or may not be a member of the Council. The contributions of the award recipients should be generally consistent with the values and mission of the CTBUH and its founder, Dr. Lynn S. Beedle. The awards are not intended to be awarded posthumously, although they may be so awarded in some cases.

Fazlur Khan Medal

The award recognizes an individual for his/her demonstrated excellence in technical design and/or research that has made a significant contribution to a discipline(s) for the design of tall buildings and the built urban environment. The contribution may be demonstrated in the form of specific technical advances, innovations, design breakthroughs, building systems integration or innovative engineering systems that resulted in a practical design solution and completion of a project(s). The consideration may be based on a single project or creative achievement through multiple projects.

Opposite: From left to right: Lynn S. Beedle – CTBUH Founder; William Pedersen – 2010 Lynn Beedle Award winner; Fazlur Khan – CTBUH Chairman (1979–1982); Ysrael A. Seinuk – 2010 Fazlur Khan Medal winner

William Pedersen

Kohn Pedersen Fox Associates

Since the beginning of his career, William Pedersen's approach to design has been one that weds formal and technical originality with a modesty informed by a deep respect for spatial and historical context. The ability to solve design challenges in ways that contribute to, but do not depart from, the urbanism from which they are born is rare amongst architects, and perhaps even rarer amongst those working on tall buildings. This is not to say that Mr. Pedersen's approach is one limited to the sources of tradition and convention. On the contrary, he has shown remarkable ability in thoroughly understanding context, helping it to speak in new ways and to new audiences.

Mr. Pedersen's design philosophy embraces the relationship between internal and external elements,

focusing on the connection of the building and its surrounding community. His work evokes response by drawing together the past and the present, striving to embody both memory and invention.

In projects ranging from small residential buildings to supertall towers, Mr. Pedersen demonstrates the power that buildings have to affect the communities in which they reside, and their ability to influence the lives of those who live and work within them. This endows the architect with great responsibility.

After getting his Master of Architecture degree from MIT in 1963, Mr. Pedersen worked as a designer with Pietro Belluschi in 1963 and with Eduardo Catalano from 1964 to 1965. He studied at the American Academy in Rome as a recipient of the Rome Prize in Architecture in 1965, and was an associate with I.M. Pei and Partners from 1967 to 1971, after which he became Vice President of John Carl Warnecke and Associates for five years. In 1976, he co-founded Kohn Pedersen Fox Associates with A. Eugene Kohn and Sheldon Fox.

Mr. Pedersen's first project, 333 Wacker Drive (1983) in Chicago, remains one of the city's most celebrated buildings, demonstrating that the best way to truly respect site context is to take full advantage of its unique character and to allow it to inform the entire design process. At a site where urban grid meets curved river, the context suggests a design that addresses two distinct sides. According to The Chicago

Opposite: International Commerce Centre, Hong Kong, China, (2010). Recognized by the CTBUH as the fourth tallest building in the world at the time of its completion – 484m (1,588ft)

"Pedersen's ability to scale his towers into a city's
fabric demonstrates an uncommon concern for urban

Left: 333 Wacker Drive, Chicago, USA (1983)
Right: DG Bank Headquarters, Frankfurt, Germany (1993)
Opposite: One of Pedersen's concept sketches for the
Shanghai World Financial Center

Tribune's Blair Kamin, "333 Wacker Drive adapts to the city's essence. The curving green glass office building that gracefully marks a bend in the Chicago River made stars of its New York City architects and helped introduce postmodernism to Chicago."

Similarly, Mr. Pedersen's design for the DG Bank Headquarters (1993) in Frankfurt, Germany, responds to the complexities of the site with one side facing a low-rise residential district and the other facing the CBD. The tower's central spine anchors the building on the Frankfurt skyline while formal divisions and fractures correspond to neighboring towers. Its narrowest dimension faces the residential neighborhood and opens up office views to the city, with massing scaled to connect to the low-rise residential neighborhood. The Shanghai World Financial Center (2008) has been heralded as a symbol of commerce and culture that speaks to the emergence of Shanghai as a global city, and was the CTBUH's recipient of the Best Tall Building "Overall" Award in 2008. At a height of 492m (1,614ft) it was recognized by the CTBUH as the second tallest building in the world at the time of its completion. To date it still holds the title of the world's highest observation deck, which at 474m (1,555ft) is 22m (72ft) higher than the observatory at the Burj Khalifa. The Shanghai World Financial Center's design is that of a square prism intersected by two cosmic arcs—ancient Chinese symbols representing the heavens and the earth. The interaction between these two realms gives rise to the building's form, which features a sky portal carved out of the top of the tower, lending balance to the structure and linking the two opposing elements.

Pedersen's recently completed International Commerce Centre (2010), located in Hong Kong, became the world's fourth tallest building at the time of its completion at a height of 484m (1,588ft). Poised at the tip of Victoria Harbor, the tower's subtly tapered re-entrant corners and the gently sloped curves at its base are designed to optimize its structural performance. These curves splay out at the base of the tower, rooting the tower in its surroundings, while creating sheltering canopies on three sides, and a dramatic atrium on the north side. The atrium gestures towards the rest of the Union Square development and serves as a public connection space for retail and rail station functions. *(Note: This project was not submitted for consideration for a CTBUH 2010 Award and thus does not feature in this book. It is expected that this building will be submitted for consideration for the CTBUH 2011 Awards program.)*

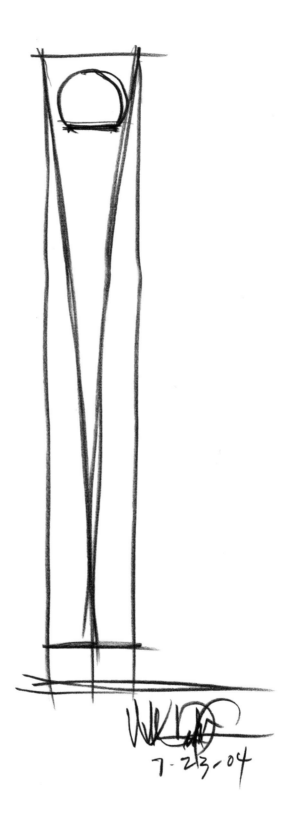

Jury Statement

For his achievements in architecture and the establishment of one of the world's most celebrated firms, Bill Pedersen is one of our most significant practitioners in the field of architecture today. For the last 34 years, under his design leadership, KPF has contributed to the advancement and innovation of architecture through its global practice. His contribution to the design of tall buildings is embodied in the consistent quality and sheer excellence of his vast portfolio of significant urban towers. His influence is immense and ubiquitous.

Mr. Pedersen's philosophy on tall building design and deep interest in natural form have created everlasting images that have changed and influenced the skylines of most major cities around the globe. He designs intuitively—not by computer calculations—but by carving out forms from damp clay in the age old methods of the grand masters.

> ## "Mr. Pedersen derives most of his designs to reflect on the city's culture, its contextual setting, and most importantly, he creates a dialogue with adjacent buildings."
>
> *Ahmad Abdelrazaq, Juror, Samsung Corporation*

Each building designed by Mr. Pedersen has its own personality yet all his buildings are dedicated to creating a dialogue with their surroundings. His designs exemplify the belief that the art of architecture and the art of urbanism are inseparable and that when a KPF structure is completed, the client has made a contribution not only to its own future, but the future of a city as well. According to Rafael Viñoly, "His contribution spans continents, from Asia to the Americas and Europe, not only as a designer and creator of urban form but also a leader and mentor ... I have known and admired him personally and professionally for over 20 years. Bill's designs have transcended generations in time without appearing dated."

For his achievements and contributions to the built environment, Mr. Pedersen has personally received six AIA National Chapter Honor Awards and numerous Merit, Design Excellence and Distinguished Architecture Awards from various AIA state and city chapters. He was awarded the Gold Medal for lifetime achievement in architecture from Tau Sigma Delta, the National Honor Society for Architecture and the Allied Arts, and the Arnold W. Brunner Memorial Prize in Architecture for Contributions in Architecture as an Art, awarded by the American Academy and the Institute of Arts and Letters. Mr. Pedersen lectures and has served on academic and professional juries and symposia throughout the world.

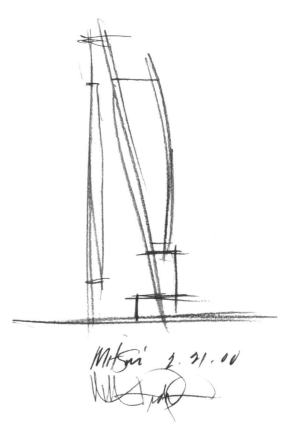

Ysrael A. Seinuk

Ysrael A. Seinuk, PC

In 1954, Ysrael Seinuk graduated from the school of Engineering at the University of Havana. In 1960 he emigrated to the United States. Today Professor Seinuk can look back on five decades of creative innovation, a remarkable portfolio of structures, a renowned teaching career and an impressive catalog of awards. He has been privileged to work with numerous world-class architects.

When Professor Seinuk opened his first practice in Havana he designed several important projects in Cuba, among them the 50-story Edificio Libertad and a 50-story concrete building with Martin Dominguez, a renowned Spanish architect. It was at this time that he presented the owners with the concept of a "megastructure" to be built over an existing theater, supported by four columns, with a superstructure composed of seven independent, seven-story buildings supported by mega-columns and mega-beams. However, the project never reached the building stage, struck down by the Castro Revolution.

It took years before Professor Seinuk could actually put his "megastructure" system to use. It was incorporated into the design of 450 Lexington Avenue in New York City, a high-rise tower built above and through a landmark post office building with the additional complication of being situated directly above congested storage tracks under Grand Central Station. The key to the structural solution was the use of four mega columns forming the "legs of a table" which carry the tower's gravity and wind loads within the existing building's shell. The mega column sizes were governed by the available space between the tracks. The mega truss "table top" picked up all of the tower's columns and transferred their load to the mega columns and twelve strategically located conventional steel columns. The physical complexity and intricate composite behavior of the building were determined by computer modeling to control vertical and lateral movements that could impact the landmark building façade below.

In 1955, Seinuk met the renowned architect Philip Johnson who was designing the Havana Riviera Hotel. He was also the structural engineer for Johnson's famous "Lipstick Building" in New York City. Decades later, when it came to building the final signature

Opposite: Trump World Tower, New York, USA, (2001). This was the tallest all-residential tower in the world at the time of its completion – 262m (861ft)

"Mr. Seinuk's ability to develop efficient, economical, and well-integrated structural solutions is easily seen in his work."

Ahmad Abdelrazaq, Juror, Samsung Corporation

Left: Edificio Libertad, Havana, Cuba (Designed:1958)
Right: 53rd at Third, the "Lipstick Building,"
New York, USA (1986)
Opposite Top: Structural diagram of 450 Lexington
Avenue, New York, USA (1991)
Opposite Bottom: 4 Times Square, New York, USA (1999)

structure in the Johnson estate—the "Gatehouse" (1995)—that would stand as a commemoration of Johnson's life, he chose Seinuk to design its structure.

As a consequence of the Castro Revolution, all private work in Cuba came to a halt. In 1959 Professor Seinuk was invited by the Minister of Public Works to organize the Ministry's Department of Structures and he and his team were charged with designing all types of buildings, bridges and infrastructure. At the same time he entered a competition for a teaching position at the University of Havana becoming the youngest instructor to teach structures at the university. This began a teaching career that he continues to this day as a professor of structural design at the Cooper Union School of Architecture where he heads the Structural

Department and the Academic Standards Committee. Since his arrival in the U.S., Professor Seinuk has been pioneering concepts in high-rise building design. Currently, his firm Ysrael A. Seinuk, PC, established in 1977, is designing major public and private projects worldwide. Many of Professor Seinuk's most notable high-rise buildings, many of which were undertaken whilst Chief Executive of Cantor Seinuk (later acquired by WSP), have had a significant impact on the New York skyline including: 919 Third Avenue, the first building in New York City with a concrete core and a steel structure; Park Lane North and South, where he introduced the use in New York of multi-strand post tensioning in order to support a 24-story building over a 19.5m (64ft) clear span; 520 Madison Avenue, with its distinctive sloping façade; the iconic

Time Warner Center; 4 Times Square, dubbed the first green skyscraper in New York; the hexagonal 383 Madison Avenue Tower; and Trump World Tower, the most slender and tallest concrete high-rise building at the time it was built.

Trump World Tower, a $400 million, 81,755 sq m (880,000 sq ft) building rises 262m (861ft) above street level with two underground levels. The tower footprint is rectangular with a 23.5m x 44m (77ft x 144ft) dimension. This provides a slenderness ratio of 11:1, which in combination with its height, defines its principal engineering challenge. The building is a concrete structure with major shear walls providing the lateral resisting system. The stiffness of the shear walls are enhanced by a perimeter concrete "belt" at the mid-height of the tower and a perimeter concrete "hat" at the roof of the building. In order to minimize wind induced acceleration, the tower's tuned mass damper system was incorporated into the design. The building was recognized with four engineering awards including an ACEC National Award and their regional Diamond Award.

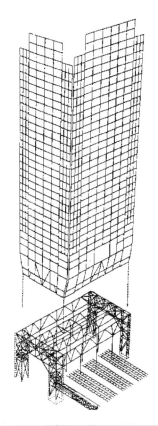

Jury Statement

One can hardly look upon the New York City skyline without seeing the influence of Mr. Seinuk's engineering, having developed the structural systems for many of the city's high-rise buildings. Going back even to his earliest works in Cuba, his vast contribution to structural and civil engineering projects is clearly evident and has elevated his firm and himself into one of the great leaders in the field of engineering.

Throughout Mr. Seinuk's career he has shown his natural ability to be innovative in developing efficient and economical structural solutions in challenging situations. His keen ability to accomplish this by using well-integrated solutions that complement and enhance the architecture is clearly evidenced in his vast body of work. His involvement in practice and a long term commitment to teaching clearly demonstrates his passion to the structural engineering profession.

> ## "One of the great leaders in the field of engineering—especially in his high-rise work—Mr. Seinuk has influenced and mentored a generation of engineers."
>
> *Gordon Gill, Awards Chair, Adrian Smith + Gordon Gill Architecture*

Beyond his home base of New York City, examples of Professor Seinuk's high-rise buildings are the Mellon Bank Tower in Philadelphia with a distinctive post tension system used to eliminate several existing columns that were supporting the street; Met Complex in Miami designed to be a 74-story residential building, a 48-story office building and a 44-story hotel over 13-stories of parking, and the Empire World Tower, two 110-story high-rises planned for downtown Miami that reached the design development phase before local economic conditions held up the project. Some international projects include the award winning Torre Mayor in Mexico City; Panorama City in Bratislava; the 320m (1,050ft) tall plot 41 building in Dubai, UAE and the award-winning O14 with its elegant structural exoskeleton, also in Dubai.

Professor Seinuk has received over 100 project, professional and personal awards, including ENR's Men Who Made Marks and the ASCE Homer Gage Balcom Award, and has been recognized for his impact on high-rise building design not only by his peers but also in the general press, having been dubbed "the Master Builder" by Time Magazine in August of 2005 in its front page feature "The 25 Most Influential Hispanics in America."

CTBUH Fellows are recognized for their contribution to the Council over an extended period of time, and in recognition of their work and sharing of their knowledge in the design and construction of tall buildings and the urban habitat.

Thomas J. McCool
Turner International LLC, USA

Mr. McCool has over 50 years experience as a leader in the construction industry, with more than 20 years in international construction markets. Tom's career has included involvement in Senior Management positions for firms providing Project Management, Construction Management, Design Build, Turn-key Development, and General Contracting. Tom has been active for more than 25 years with the CTBUH, involved in several committees. He was the chair of the Development and Management Working Group until 2000, and is currently serving in the Council's Advisory Group.

Moira Moser
M. Moser Associates, Hong Kong

Founding M. Moser Associates in 1981, Ms. Moser's firm is the largest in Asia focusing on design and delivery of corporate interior architecture. The firm's capabilities have recently expanded to include solutions for large-scale facilities and campuses, and complex engineering-intensive facilities. Her involvement with the CTBUH spans over 20 years. She served on two Awards Committees, was Vice-Chair of the Interior Design Committee until 2000, was a Conference Organizer for the 1997 Hong Kong Conference, and is currently serving in the Council's Advisory Group.

Shankar Nair
Teng & Associates, USA

A structural engineer with a focus on large architectural and civil engineering projects, Dr. Nair was inducted into the National Academy of Engineering in 2005 for his "contributions to the art and science of engineering through the design of innovative bridges and building structures." Dr. Nair had his first experience with the Council in 1972 as a Conference attendee, became increasingly active in the mid-1980s, eventually serving as the eighth Chairman of the Council from 1997–2001.

Gordon Gill, *Awards Committee Chair 2009–2010, Adrian Smith + Gordon Gill Architecture,* Chicago, USA

Gordon's work emphasizes a holistic approach to design that integrates all project disciplines. The results are performance-based designs that work symbiotically with their natural surroundings. His work includes the design of civic facilities, large-scale mixed-use developments, city-wide master plans and the world's intended first net Zero-Energy skyscraper, Pearl River Tower.

Ahmad Abdelrazaq, *Samsung Corporation,* Seoul, South Korea

As Executive Vice President of the High-rise Building and Structural Engineering Divisions at Samsung C & T Corporation, Ahmad has been involved in many high-rise projects, including the Jin Mao Tower in Shanghai, and the 151-story Incheon Tower, Incheon, South Korea. Ahmad serves as adjunct professor at Seoul National University and chairman of the ASCE/SEI tall buildings committee.

Bruce Kuwabara, *KPMB Architects,* Toronto, Canada

A founding partner of KPMB, Bruce is an advocate of design quality for city building, and is known both for creating architecture that enriches the public realm and as a spokesperson on issues of urbanism and the contemporary city. He was the architect of Manitoba Hydro Place, CTBUH's 2009 Best Tall Building Americas winner.

Peter Murray, *Wordsearch/New London Architecture Centre,* London, UK

Peter trained as an architect but has spent much of his career as a writer and communicator. He is the Director of the New London Architecture Centre which is the focus for debate and discussion of issues relating to development in the British capital. He founded the design and architecture magazine Blueprint and he is chairman of Wordsearch a global marketing company specialising in architecture and real estate.

Matthias Schuler, *Transsolar ClimateEngineering,* Stuttgart, Germany

Matthias is founder of Transsolar, a climate engineering firm whose scope is to ensure the highest possible comfort in the built environment with the lowest possible impact on the environment. Matthias works with architects on international projects giving focus on new energy-saving and comfort-optimizing strategies by an integral approach to building design.

Mun Summ Wong, *WOHA Architects,* Singapore

Mun Summ is a co-founding director of WOHA, a regional design practice based in Singapore which has extensive experience in a wide range of projects around the Asia Pacific region. The practice explores integrated design for the built environment. Rather than develop a house style, WOHA focuses on the architectural potentials within each project and acquires a formal language around these.

Antony Wood, *Council on Tall Buildings and Urban Habitat/Illinois Institute of Technology,* Chicago, USA

Antony is Executive Director of the CTBUH, responsible for the day-to-day running of the Council. His field of specialism is the design, and in particular the sustainable design, of tall buildings. Based at the College of Architecture, Illinois Institute of Technology, Antony is also an associate professor there and leads an annual "Tall & Green" building design studio.

Review of Past Winners

Previous Lynn S. Beedle Award Recipients:

2002: Dr. Lynn Beedle

2003: Charles DeBenedittis

2004: Gerald Hines

2005: Dr. Alan Davenport

2006: Dr. Ken Yeang

2007: Lord Norman Foster

2008: Cesar Pelli

2009: John C. Portman, Jr.

Previous Fazlur Khan Medal Recipients:

2004: Leslie E. Robertson

2005: Dr. Werner Sobek

2006: Srinivasa "Hal" Iyengar

2007: Dr. Farzad Naeim

2008: William F. Baker

2009: Dr. Prabodh V. Banavalkar

Previous Best Tall Building Award Recipients:

2009 Winners:

Best Tall Building – Overall & Best Tall Building Asia & Australasia
Linked Hybrid
Beijing, China

Best Tall Building – Americas
Manitoba Hydro Place
Winnipeg, Canada

Best Tall Building – Europe
The Broadgate Tower
London, UK

Best Tall Building – Middle East & Africa
Tornado Tower
Doha, Qatar

2008 Winners:

Best Tall Building – Overall & Best Tall Building Asia & Australasia
Shanghai World Financial Center
Shanghai, China

Best Tall Building – Americas
The New York Times Building
New York City, USA

Best Tall Building – Europe
51 Lime Street
London, UK

Best Tall Building – Middle East & Africa
Bahrain World Trade Center
Manama, Bahrain

2007 Winners:

Best Tall Building – Overall
Beetham Hilton Tower
Manchester, UK

Best Sustainable Tall Building
Hearst Tower
New York City, USA

Review of CTBUH 2009 Awards and 8ᵗʰ Annual Awards Dinner

The 8th Annual Awards Dinner and Ceremony was held in conjunction with the CTBUH 2009 Chicago Conference, and took place on the first evening of the conference, October 22nd, at the Illinois Institute of Technology campus in Chicago, USA. The event honored the individual lifetime achievement winners and recognized the team effort of the companies involved in each of the winning tall building projects.

Taking place in Mies van der Rohe's historic Crown Hall, the space was filled to capacity with an international audience of 380 conference delegates and guests. Table sponsors for the event included: Arup, Viracon, Walsh Construction, KONE, Skidmore, Owings & Merrill LLP, CICO Consultants, AECOM, SmithCarter/KPMB Architects, Illinois Institute of Technology, Perkins + Will, Gensler, John Portman & Associates, Rolf Jensen & Associates, Goettsch Partners, Turner Construction, the Korean Council on Tall Buildings and Urban Habitat, and Thornton Tomasetti.

Following a cocktail reception, guests took their seats to watch the acceptance of the Lifetime Achievement Awards by John Portman of John Portman & Associates and Prabodh Banavalkar of Ingenium, Inc. Mr. Portman was awarded the Lynn S. Beedle Award for his careful urban planning and ability to weave art, nature, and the pedestrian experience together in his tall building designs. Dr. Banavalkar was awarded the Fazlur Khan Medal for his ability for finding the optimum structure with due consideration to cost effectiveness, constructability, redundancy, and seamless integration with the architectural design concept. The CTBUH also recognized three new Fellows for 2009: Mir M. Ali, University of Illinois Urbana-Champaign; Irwin Cantor, Irwin G. Cantor Consultants; and Ryszard M. Kowalczyk, Bialystok University of Technology. CTBUH Fellows are

Top: Attendees enjoy the pre-dinner cocktail hour in S. R. Crown Hall
Middle: John Portman accepts the Lynn S. Beedle Award
Bottom: Prabodh Banavalkar accepts the Fazlur Khan Medal

Top: 380 Attendees are seated for the Ceremony & Dinner in Mies van der Rohe's S.R. Crown Hall, Chicago
Bottom: From left to right: Tom Gouldsborough of Manitoba Hydro accepts the Best Tall Building Americas award for Manitoba Hydo Place, Winnipeg; Jeffery McCarthy and Timothy Poell of Skidmore, Owings & Merrill LLP accept the Best Tall Building Europe award for The Broadgate Tower, London; Said Abu Odeh of QIPCO accepts the Best Tall Building Middle East & Africa award from CTBUH Executive Director, Antony Wood, for Tornado Tower, Doha

> ## "Rich in thought, both in program and architecture, offering an advanced typology for dense urban living—beautiful."
>
> *Gordon Gill, 2009 Awards Chair, on the 2009 Best Tall Building Overall, Linked Hybrid, Beijing*

recognized for their contribution to the Council over an extended period of time, and in recognition of their work and sharing of their knowledge in the design and construction of tall buildings and the urban habitat.

Following the dinner service, brief presentations were made by each of the regional Best Tall Building winners as they came up onto the stage to accept their awards. Manitoba Hydro Place (Winnipeg, Canada) won the award for Best Tall Building Americas, and was accepted by building owner Tom Gouldsborough of Manitoba Hydro and architect Bruce Kuwabara of KPMB Architects. Linked Hybrid (Beijing, China) won for Best Tall Building Asia & Australasia and was accepted by design architect Steven Holl of Steven Holl

Architects. The Broadgate Tower (London, UK) won for Best Tall Building Europe, accepted by architects Timothy Poell and Jeffery McCarthy of Skidmore, Owings & Merrill LLP. Tornado Tower (Doha, Qatar) won for Best Tall Building Middle East & Africa and was accepted by building owner Said Abu Odeh of QIPCO.

After the presentations, CTBUH Awards Committee Chairman, Gordon Gill, of Adrian Smith + Gordon Gill Architecture, invited Illinois Institute of Technology Provost and Senior Vice President for Academic Affairs, Alan Cramb onto the stage for the honor of revealing the Best Tall Building Overall for 2009. Taking the sealed envelope from Gordon, Mr. Cramb

took the podium and with all the flourish of a typical awards show, broke the seal of the envelope with the words, "And the winner is…" The suspense in the audience was tangible, but without further delay it was revealed that the Overall winner was Linked Hybrid. Architect Steven Holl returned to the stage to claim the big prize for the evening. Looking noticeably surprised and excited, Mr. Holl gave a few words of acceptance. Joining Mr. Holl on stage was Li Hu, project manager in Beijing from Steven Holl Architects, Congzhen Xiao, from structural engineer on the project, China Academy of Building Research, and Stefan Holst, from environmental consultants, Transsolar ClimateEngineering.

While accepting the award, Mr. Holl admitted that while he was honored by the recognition he couldn't help but be surprised at the win because Linked Hybrid is only 22 stories tall. CTBUH Executive director and 2009 Awards Jury member, Antony Wood was later quoted with the following response: "Though Linked Hybrid is not especially tall (though it certainly meets the Council's criteria for defining a tall building), it points the way forward for the intensified multi-use, multi-level, connected cities of the future."

The evening ended with the official end of David Scott's term as CTBUH Chairman. Serving since 2006, David passed the Chairmanship to Professor Sang Dae Kim by literally passing the CTBUH Gavel onto him. Professor Kim gave a brief speech on his vision for the future of the Council. David was then presented with an honorary plaque for his services and treated to a light hearted tribute video which drew chuckles from the crowd.

The Council is the official arbiter of the criteria upon which tall building height is measured, and thus the title of "The World's Tallest Building" determined. The Council maintains an extensive set of definitions and criteria for measuring and classifying tall buildings. These criteria are the basis for the information found in the "data boxes" on each project throughout this book, and on the "100 Tallest Buildings in the World" list (see pages 188–191).

What is a Tall Building?

There is no absolute definition of what constitutes a "tall building." It is a building that exhibits some element of "tallness" in one or more of the following categories:

a) Height relative to context: It is not just about height, but about the context in which it exists. Thus whereas a 14-story building may not be considered a tall building in a high-rise city such as Chicago or Hong Kong, in a provincial European city or a suburb this may be distinctly taller than the urban norm.

b) Proportion: Again, a tall building is not just about height but also about proportion. There are numerous buildings which are not particularly high, but are slender enough to give the appearance of a tall building, especially against low urban backgrounds. Conversely, there are numerous big/large footprint buildings which are quite tall but their size/floor area rules them out as being classed as a tall building.

c) Tall Building Technologies: If a building contains technologies which may be attributed as being a product of "tall" (e.g., specific vertical transport technologies, structural wind bracing as a product of height, etc.), then this building can be classed as a tall building.

Although number of floors is a poor indicator of defining a tall building due to the changing floor to floor height between differing buildings and functions (e.g., office versus residential usage), a building of perhaps 14 or more stories (or over 50 meters/165 feet in height) could perhaps be used as a threshold for considering it a "tall building."

What is a Supertall Building?

Again, opinions on this differ internationally. Although great heights are now being achieved with built tall buildings (in excess of 800 meters/2600 feet), at the start of 2010 there were only 42 buildings in excess of 300 meters completed and occupied globally. The CTBUH thus defines "supertall" as being any building over 300 meters/984 feet in height.

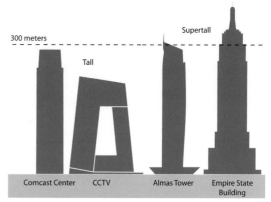

Diagram of tall vs. supertall

How is a tall building measured?

The CTBUH recognizes three different categories for the measuring of building height (see diagrams opposite):

1. Height to Architectural Top

Height is measured from the level[1] of the lowest, significant[2], open-air[3], pedestrian[4] entrance to the architectural top of the building, including spires, but not including antennae, signage, flag poles or other functional-technical equipment[5]. This measurement is the most widely utilized and is employed to define the Council on Tall Buildings and Urban Habitat rankings of the "World's Tallest Buildings."

World's tallest 10 buildings according to Height to Architectural Top (as of July 2010)

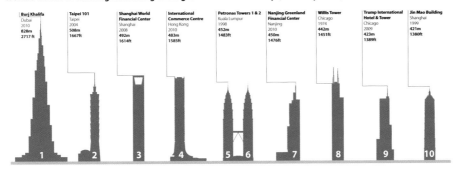

World's tallest 10 buildings according to Highest Occupied Floor (as of July 2010)

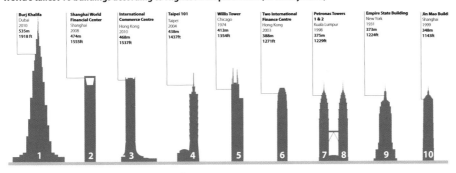

World's tallest 10 buildings according to Height to Tip (as of July 2010)

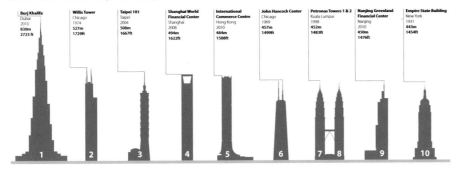

2. Highest Occupied Floor

Height is measured from the level[1] of the lowest, significant[2], open-air[3], pedestrian[4] entrance to the highest occupied[6] floor within the building.

3. Height to Tip

Height is measured from the level[1] of the lowest, significant[2], open-air[3], pedestrian[4] entrance to the highest point of the building, irrespective of material or function of the highest element (i.e., including antennae, flagpoles, signage and other functional-technical equipment).

Floor Number:

The number of floors should include the ground floor level and be the number of main floors above ground, including any significant mezzanine floors and major mechanical plant floors. Mechanical mezzanines should not be included if they have a significantly smaller floor area than the major floors below. Similarly, mechanical penthouses or plant rooms protruding above the general roof area should not be counted. Note: CTBUH floor counts may differ from published accounts, as it is common in some regions of the world for certain floor levels not to be included (e.g., the level 4, 14, 24, etc. in Hong Kong).

Building Usage:

What is the difference between a tall building and a telecommunications/observation tower?

A tall "building" can be classed as such (as opposed to a telecommunications/observation tower) and is eligible for the "Tallest" lists if at least 50% of its height is occupied by usable floor area.

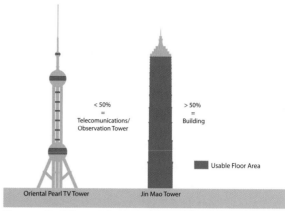

Diagram of building vs. telecommunications/observation towers

Single-Function and Mixed-Use buildings

A **single-function** tall building is defined as one where 85% or more of its total floor area is dedicated to a single usage. A **mixed-use** tall building contains two or more functions (or uses), where each of the functions occupy a significant proportion[7] of the tower's total space. Support areas such as car parks and mechanical plant space do not constitute mixed-use functions. Functions are denoted on CTBUH "Tallest" lists in descending order, e.g., "hotel/office" indicates hotel function above office function.

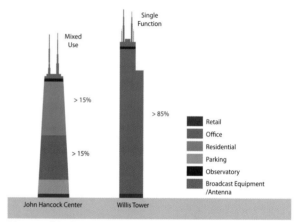

Diagram of single vs. mixed-use towers

Building Status:

When is a tall building considered to be "completed"?

A completed building can be considered such—and added to the "Tallest" lists—if it fulfills all of the following three criteria: 1) topped out structurally and architecturally, 2) fully-clad, 3) open for business, or at least partially occupied.

When is a tall building considered to be "topped out" architecturally?

A tall building is "topped out" architecturally when it has reached its ultimate architectural height (e.g., it includes spires, parapets, etc).

When is a tall building considered to be "under construction"?

A tall building is considered to be "under construction" when site clearing has been completed and foundation/piling work has begun.

When is a tall building labeled as "construction stopped"?

A tall building is labeled as "construction stopped" when it is widely reported within the public domain that construction has halted.

When is a tall building considered to be a "real" proposal?

A "real" proposed tall building can be considered such if it fulfills ALL of the following criteria: 1) Has a specific site, 2) Has a developer/financier who owns the site, 3) Has a full professional design team who are in the process of progressing the design beyond the conceptual stage, 4) Has a dialogue with the local planning authorities with a view to obtaining full legal permission for construction, 5) Has a full intention to progress the building to construction and completion.

Only buildings that have been announced publically by the client and fulfill all the above criteria will be included in the CTBUH "proposed" building listings. Also, note that due to the changing nature of early stage designs and client information restrictions, some height data for "proposed" tall buildings that appears on the CTBUH "Tallest" lists is unconfirmed.

Structural Material:
A **steel** tall building is defined as one where the main vertical and lateral structural elements and floor systems are constructed from steel.

A **concrete** tall building is defined as one where the main vertical and lateral structural elements and floor systems are constructed from concrete.

A **composite** tall building utilizes a combination of both steel and concrete acting compositely in the main structural elements, thus including a steel building with a concrete core.

A **mixed-structure** tall building is any building that utilizes distinct steel or concrete systems above or below each other. There are two main types of mixed structural systems: A **steel/concrete** tall building indicates a steel structural system located above a concrete structural system, with the opposite true of a **concrete/steel** building.

Additional Notes on Material:
1) If a tall building is of steel construction with a floor system of concrete planks on steel beams, it is considered a steel tall building.
2) If a tall building is of steel construction with a floor system of a concrete slab on steel beams, it is considered a steel tall building.
3) If a tall building has steel columns plus a floor system of concrete beams, it is considered a composite tall building.

Determination of Compliance to Criteria:
Due to the complex and diverse nature of tall building designs worldwide, some exceptions to this set of criteria may be appropriate depending on the particular building. The CTBUH Height Committee therefore reserves the right to examine and define such exceptions on a case by case basis.

Footnotes:

[1] Level: finished floor level at threshold of the lowest entrance door.

[2] Significant: the entrance should be predominantly above existing or pre-existing grade and permit access to one or more primary uses in the building via elevators, as opposed to ground floor retail or other uses which solely relate/connect to the immediately adjacent external environment. Thus entrances via below-grade sunken plazas or similar are not generally recognized. Also note that access to car park and/or ancillary/support areas are not considered significant entrances.

[3] Open-air: the entrance must be located directly off of an external space at that level that is open to air.

[4] Pedestrian: refers to common building users or occupants and is intended to exclude service, ancillary, or similar areas.

[5] Functional-technical equipment: this is intended to recognize that functional-technical equipment is subject to removal/addition/change as per prevalent technologies, as is often seen in tall buildings (e.g., antennae, signage, wind turbines, etc. are periodically added, shortened, lengthened, removed and/or replaced).

[6] Highest occupied floor: this is intended to recognize conditioned space which is designed to be safely and legally occupied by residents, workers or other building users on a consistent basis. It does not include service or mechanical areas which experience occasional maintenance access, etc.

[7] This "significant proportion" can be judged as 15% or greater of either: (1) the total floor area, or (2) the total building height, in terms of number of floors occupied for the function. However, care should be taken in the case of supertall towers. For example a 20-story hotel function as part of a 150-story tower does not comply with the 15% rule, though this would clearly constitute mixed-use.

100 Tallest Buildings in the World as of July 2010

The Council maintains the list of the 100 Tallest Buildings in the world, which are ranked based on the height to architectural top, and includes not only completed buildings, but also buildings currently under construction. However, a building does not receive an official ranking number until it is completed.

Color Key:

Buildings listed in black are completed and officially ranked by the CTBUH.

Buildings listed in green are under construction and have topped out.

Buildings listed in red are under construction, but have not yet topped out.

Rank	Building Name	City	Year	Stories	Height (m)	Height (ft)	Material	Use
1	Burj Khalifa	Dubai	2010	163	828	2717	steel/concrete	office/residential/hotel
	Ping An International Finance Center Tower 1	Shenzhen	2015	115	648	2126	–	office
	Shanghai Tower	Shanghai	2014	128	632	2074	composite	hotel/office/exhibition/retail
	Goldin Finance 117	Tianjin	2014	117	597	1959	composite	hotel/office
	Makkah Royal Clock Tower Hotel	Makkah	2011	85	591	1939	steel/concrete	hotel
	One World Trade Center	New York	2013	105	541	1776	composite	office
	Pentominium	Dubai	2013	122	516	1692	steel/concrete	residential
	Qatar National Bank Tower	Doha	2013	101	510	1673	–	office
2	Taipei 101	Taipei	2004	101	508	1667	composite	office
3	Shanghai World Financial Center	Shanghai	2008	101	492	1614	composite	hotel/office
4	International Commerce Centre	Hong Kong	2010	108	484	1588	composite	hotel/office
5	Petronas Tower 1	Kuala Lumpur	1998	88	452	1483	composite	office
5	Petronas Tower 2	Kuala Lumpur	1998	88	452	1483	composite	office
7	Nanjing Greenland Financial Center	Nanjing	2010	66	450	1476	composite	hotel/office
8	Willis Tower	Chicago	1974	108	442	1451	steel	office
	Kingkey Finance Tower	Shenzhen	2012	98	442	1449	composite	hotel/office
	Guangzhou International Finance Center	Guangzhou	2010	103	441	1446	composite	hotel/office
	Dubai Towers Doha	Doha	2012	91	437	1432	concrete	residential/office/hotel
9	Trump International Hotel & Tower	Chicago	2009	98	423	1389	concrete	residential/hotel
10	Jin Mao Building	Shanghai	1999	88	421	1380	composite	hotel/office
	Princess Tower	Dubai	2011	101	414	1358	concrete	residential
	Al Hamra Tower	Kuwait City	2010	77	413	1354	concrete	office
	Marina 101	Dubai	2012	101	412	1352	concrete	residential/hotel
11	Two International Finance Centre	Hong Kong	2003	88	412	1352	composite	office
	Two World Trade Center	New York	–	79	411	1348	composite	office
12	CITIC Plaza	Guangzhou	1996	80	390	1280	concrete	office
	23 Marina	Dubai	2011	90	389	1276	concrete	residential
	Eton Place Dalian Tower 1	Dalian	2013	81	388	1274	composite	hotel/office
	Diamond Tower	Jeddah	–	83	388	1273	–	residential
	Forum 66 Tower 1	Shenyang	2013	76	384	1260	–	office
13	Shun Hing Square	Shenzhen	1996	69	384	1260	composite	office
	The Domain	Abu Dhabi	2012	88	381	1251	concrete	residential
14	Empire State Building	New York	1931	102	381	1250	steel	office
	Elite Residence	Dubai	2011	87	381	1250	concrete	residential
	Mercury City Tower	Moscow	2011	70	380	1247	concrete	hotel/office
	Three World Trade Center	New York	2014	71	378	1240	composite	office
	Emirates Park Towers Hotel & Spa 1	Dubai	2011	77	376	1234	concrete	residential/hotel
	Emirates Park Towers Hotel & Spa 2	Dubai	2011	77	376	1234	concrete	residential/hotel
15	Central Plaza	Hong Kong	1992	78	374	1227	concrete	office
16	Bank of China Tower	Hong Kong	1989	70	367	1205	composite	office
17	Bank of America Tower	New York	2009	55	366	1200	composite	office
18	Almas Tower	Dubai	2008	68	360	1181	concrete	office
	The Pinnacle	Guangzhou	2011	60	360	1181	concrete	office
	Sinosteel International Tower	Tianjin	2013	80	358	1175	–	office
19	Emirates Tower One	Dubai	2000	54	355	1163	composite	office
	Forum 66 Tower 2	Shenyang	2013	68	351	1150	–	office
	Gezhouba International Plaza	Wuhan	2013	69	350	1148	–	office

Rank	Building Name	City	Year	Stories	Height m	ft	Material	Use
20	Tuntex Sky Tower	Kaohsiung	1997	85	348	1140	composite	hotel/office
21	Aon Center	Chicago	1973	83	346	1136	steel	office
22	The Center	Hong Kong	1998	73	346	1135	steel	office
	The Torch	Dubai	2011	80	345	1132	concrete	residential
23	John Hancock Center	Chicago	1969	100	344	1128	steel	residential/office
	Ahmed Abdul Rahim Al Attar Tower	Dubai	2011	76	342	1122	concrete	residential
	Parc1 Tower A	Seoul	2013	68	338	1109	–	office
	Tianjin World Financial Center	Tianjin	2010	76	337	1106	composite	office
	Keangnam Hanoi Landmark Tower	Hanoi	2011	71	336	1102	concrete	hotel/residential/office
	ADNOC Headquarters	Abu Dhabi	2012	65	335	1100	–	office
24	Shimao International Plaza	Shanghai	2006	60	333	1094	concrete	hotel/office
25	Rose Rayhaan by Rotana	Dubai	2007	72	333	1093	composite	hotel
	Tianjin Kerry Center	Tianjin	2012	72	333	1093	–	office
26	Minsheng Bank Building	Wuhan	2008	68	331	1086	steel	office
	Ryugyong Hotel	Pyongyang	2012	105	330	1083	concrete	hotel
27	China World Trade Center III	Beijing	2009	74	330	1083	steel	hotel/office
	United International Mansion	Chongqing	2011	72	330	1083	concrete	office
	The Index	Dubai	2010	80	328	1076	concrete	residential/office
	Hanging Village of Huaxi	Jiangyin	2011	74	328	1076	composite	residential
	Al Yaqoub Tower	Dubai	2011	69	328	1076	concrete	residential/hotel
	Wuxi Suning Plaza 1	Wuxi	2013	68	328	1076	–	hotel/office
	The Landmark	Abu Dhabi	2011	72	324	1063	concrete	residential
	Deji Plaza Phase 2	Nanjing	2012	62	324	1063	composite	office
	Yantai Shimao No. 1 The Harbour	Yantai	2011	57	323	1060	composite	hotel/office
28	Q1	Gold Coast	2005	78	323	1058	concrete	residential
	Gate of Taipei Tower 1	Taipei	2013	76	322	1057	–	hotel/office/retail
	Lamar Tower 1	Jeddah	2013	65	322	1056	concrete	residential/office
29	Wenzhou Trade Center	Wenzhou	2010	68	322	1056	concrete	hotel/office
30	Burj al Arab Hotel	Dubai	1999	60	321	1053	composite	hotel
	Palais Royale	Mumbai	–	66	320	1050	concrete	residential
31	Chrysler Building	New York	1930	77	319	1047	steel	office
32	Nina Tower	Hong Kong	2006	80	319	1046	concrete	hotel/office
33	New York Times Tower	New York	2007	52	319	1046	steel	office
	Yingli Tower	Chongqing	2012	61	318	1043	concrete	office
34	HHHR Tower	Dubai	2010	72	318	1042	concrete	residential
35	Bank of America Plaza	Atlanta	1993	55	317	1040	composite	office
36	Sky Tower	Abu Dhabi	2010	74	312	1024	concrete	residential/office
	Ocean Heights	Dubai	2010	83	310	1017	concrete	residential
37	U.S. Bank Tower	Los Angeles	1990	73	310	1017	steel	office
38	Menara Telekom	Kuala Lumpur	2001	55	310	1017	concrete	office
	Pearl River Tower	Guangzhou	2011	71	310	1016	composite	office
39	Emirates Tower Two	Dubai	2000	56	309	1014	concrete	hotel
	City Hall and City Duma	Moscow	2013	71	308	1012	–	government/office
	Shenyang New World International Convention & Exhibition Center Tower 1	Shenyang	2013	60	308	1010	–	office
	Shenyang New World International Convention & Exhibition Center Tower 2	Shenyang	2013	60	308	1010	–	office
40	AT&T Corporate Center	Chicago	1989	60	307	1007	composite	office
	Infinity Tower	Dubai	2011	76	306	1005	concrete	residential
	Carnegie 57	New York	2013	75	306	1005	concrete	residential/hotel
	East Pacific Center Tower A	Shenzhen	2012	85	306	1004	concrete	residential
	Shard London Bridge	London	2012	66	306	1003	composite	residential/hotel/office
41	JPMorgan Chase Tower	Houston	1982	75	305	1002	composite	office
	Etihad Tower 2	Abu Dhabi	2010	79	305	1002	concrete	residential
42	Northeast Asia Trade Tower	Incheon	2010	68	305	1001	composite	residential/hotel/office
43	Baiyoke Tower II	Bangkok	1997	85	304	997	concrete	hotel
44	Two Prudential Plaza	Chicago	1990	64	303	995	concrete	office
	Diwang International Fortune Center	Liuzhou	2013	75	303	994	–	residential/hotel/office

Rank	Building Name	City	Year	Stories	Height m	ft	Material	Use
	Leatop Plaza	Guangzhou	2011	64	303	994	composite	office
45	Wells Fargo Plaza	Houston	1983	71	302	992	steel	office
46	Kingdom Centre	Riyadh	2002	41	302	992	steel/concrete	residential/hotel/office
47	The Address	Dubai	2009	63	302	991	concrete	residential/hotel
	Gramercy Residences	Makati	2013	68	302	991	concrete	residential
	Gate of the Orient	Suzhou	2013	68	302	990	–	residential/hotel/office
48	Capital City Moscow Tower	Moscow	2010	76	302	989	concrete	residential
	Doosan Haewundae We've the Zenith Tower A	Busan	2011	80	301	988	composite	residential
	Shenzhen Nikko Tower	Shenzhen	–	70	301	987	–	hotel/office
	Tameer Commercial Tower	Abu Dhabi	2013	74	300	984	–	office
	Dubai Pearl Tower	Dubai	2013	73	300	984	concrete	residential
	Gran Torre Costanera	Santiago	2012	70	300	984	concrete	office
49	Arraya Tower	Kuwait City	2009	60	300	984	concrete	office
	Abenobashi Terminal Tower	Osaka	2014	59	300	984	–	hotel/office/retail
50	Aspire Tower	Doha	2006	36	300	984	composite	hotel/office
51	One Island East Centre	Hong Kong	2008	69	298	979	concrete	office
52	First Bank Tower	Toronto	1975	72	298	978	steel	office
53	Shanghai Wheelock Square	Shanghai	2010	59	298	978	concrete	office
	Four World Trade Center	New York	2013	64	297	975	composite	office
54	Eureka Tower	Melbourne	2006	91	297	974	concrete	residential
55	Comcast Center	Philadelphia	2008	57	297	974	composite	office
56	Landmark Tower	Yokohama	1993	73	296	972	steel	hotel/office
57	Emirates Crown	Dubai	2008	63	296	971	concrete	residential
	Khalid Al Attar Tower 2	Dubai	2010	66	294	965	concrete	residential/office
	Islamic Bank Office Tower	Dubai	2010	49	294	964	concrete	office
	Moi City 1	Shenyang	2011	71	293	961	composite	office
	Trump Ocean Club	Panama City	2011	68	293	961	concrete	residential/hotel
	Lamar Tower 2	Jeddah	2013	59	293	961	concrete	residential/office
58	311 South Wacker Drive	Chicago	1990	65	293	961	concrete	office
	Wuxi Maoye City – Marriott Hotel	Wuxi	2011	72	292	958	–	hotel
59	SEG Plaza	Shenzhen	2000	71	292	957	concrete	hotel/office
	Haewundae I Park Marina Tower 2	Busan	2011	72	292	957	composite	residential
60	American International Building	New York	1932	67	290	952	steel	office
	Chongqing Poly Tower	Chongqing	2011	58	290	951	concrete	office/hotel
	Dongguan TBA Building	Dongguan	2011	68	289	948	composite	hotel/office
61	Key Tower	Cleveland	1991	57	289	947	composite	office
	Park Hyatt Guangzhou	Guangzhou	2013	66	289	947	–	residential/hotel/office
62	Plaza 66	Shanghai	2001	66	288	945	concrete	office
63	One Liberty Place	Philadelphia	1987	61	288	945	steel	office
	Excellence Century Plaza Tower 1	Shenzhen	2010	60	288	945	composite	office
	The Pinnacle	London	2012	64	288	945	steel	office
	SPG Global Tower 1	Suzhou	2010	54	286	938	composite	office
	SPG Global Tower 2	Suzhou	2010	54	286	938	composite	office
64	Millennium Tower	Dubai	2006	59	285	935	concrete	residential
	Sulafa Tower	Dubai	2010	75	285	935	concrete	residential
	Shimao Wulihe City Office Tower 1	Shenyang	–	–	285	935	–	office
	Shimao Wulihe City Office Tower 2	Shenyang	–	–	285	935	–	office
65	Tomorrow Square	Shanghai	2003	58	285	934	concrete	residential/hotel/office
66	Columbia Center	Seattle	1984	76	284	933	composite	office
	D1 Tower	Dubai	2011	80	284	932	concrete	residential
67	Chongqing World Trade Center	Chongqing	2005	60	283	929	concrete	office
68	Cheung Kong Centre	Hong Kong	1999	63	283	928	steel	office
69	The Trump Building	New York	1930	71	283	927	steel	office
	Doosan Haewundae We've the Zenith Tower B	Busan	2011	75	282	924	composite	residential
	Trump International Hotel & Tower	Toronto	2011	59	281	922	concrete	residential/hotel
	Catic Plaza	Shenzhen	2011	58	281	922	–	office
70	Bank of America Plaza	Dallas	1985	72	281	921	composite	office
	Torre Vitri	Panama City	2011	75	281	921	concrete	residential
71	Republic Plaza	Singapore	1995	66	280	919	composite	office
72	United Overseas Bank Plaza One	Singapore	1992	66	280	919	steel	office
73	Overseas Union Bank Centre	Singapore	1986	63	280	919	steel	office

Rank	Building Name	City	Year	Stories	Height m	ft	Material	Use
	Zhengzhou Greenland Plaza	Zhengzhou	2011	56	279	916	composite	hotel/office
	Eton Place Dalian Tower 2	Dalian	2012	62	279	915	composite	residential/office
	Three International Finance Center	Seoul	2012	55	279	915	composite	office
74	Citigroup Center	New York	1977	59	279	915	steel	office
75	Hong Kong New World Tower	Shanghai	2002	61	278	913	composite	hotel/office/retail
	Trust Tower	Abu Dhabi	2011	60	278	912	concrete	office
	Etihad Tower 1	Abu Dhabi	2010	70	278	911	concrete	residential/hotel
76	Diwang International Commerce Center	Nanning	2006	54	276	906	concrete	hotel/office
77	Scotia Tower	Toronto	1989	68	275	902	composite	office
	MAG 218 Tower	Dubai	2010	66	275	902	concrete	residential
78	Williams Tower	Houston	1983	64	275	901	steel	office
	Nantong Zhongnan International Plaza	Nantong	2011	53	273	897	steel/concrete	residential/office
79	Wuhan World Trade Tower	Wuhan	1998	60	273	896	–	office
	Lvjing Tower	Shenzhen	2011	56	273	896	concrete	–
	Shimao International Center Office Tower	Fuzhou	2013	56	273	896	–	office
	Haewundae I Park Marina Tower 1	Busan	2011	66	272	894	composite	residential
80	Renaissance Tower	Dallas	1975	56	270	886	steel	office
	Shanghai Changjiang Travel Plaza	Chongqing	2011	57	270	886	concrete	hotel/office
81	The Cullinan I	Hong Kong	2008	68	270	886	concrete	residential
81	The Cullinan II	Hong Kong	2008	68	270	886	concrete	residential/hotel
83	China International Center Tower B	Guangzhou	2007	62	270	884	concrete	office
	BHP Square	Perth	2012	46	270	884	composite	office
84	Dapeng International Plaza	Guangzhou	2006	56	269	884	composite	office
85	One Lujiazui	Shanghai	2008	47	269	883	concrete	office
	Hotel JAL Tower	Dubai	2010	60	269	883	concrete	hotel
86	21st Century Tower	Dubai	2003	55	269	883	concrete	residential
	Bitexco Financial Tower	Ho Chi Minh City	2011	68	269	882	composite	office
87	Naberezhnaya Tower C	Moscow	2007	61	268	881	composite	residential/office
	Diamond of Istanbul	Istanbul	2011	53	268	879	composite	residential/hotel/office
	Dalian Global Finance Center Tower B	Dalian	2011	53	268	879	concrete	office
	Parc1 Tower B	Seoul	2013	52	268	879	–	office
	Lotte Center	Hanoi	2013	65	267	876	–	residential/hotel/office
	Beekman Tower	New York	2011	76	267	876	concrete	residential
	Charigali Tower	Kuala Lumpur	2011	58	267	876	concrete	residential/office
88	Al Faisaliah Center	Riyadh	2000	30	267	876	steel/concrete	office
	Aura at College Park	Toronto	2014	75	266	874	concrete	residential
	The River South Tower	Bangkok	2011	73	266	871	concrete	residential
89	Bank of America Corporate Center	Charlotte	1992	60	265	871	concrete	office
	Doosan Haewundae We've the Zenith Tower C	Busan	2011	70	265	869	composite	residential
90	900 North Michigan Avenue	Chicago	1989	66	265	869	concrete/steel	residential/office/hotel/retail
91	Al Kazim Tower 1	Dubai	2008	53	265	869	concrete	residential
91	Al Kazim Tower 2	Dubai	2008	53	265	869	concrete	residential
	WBC The Palace 1	Busan	2011	51	265	869	concrete	residential
	WBC The Palace 2	Busan	2011	51	265	869	concrete	residential
93	BOCOM Financial Towers	Shanghai	1999	50	265	869	concrete	office
94	120 Collins Street	Melbourne	1991	52	265	869	concrete	office
95	Triumph Palace	Moscow	2005	61	264	866	concrete	residential
	Arts Tower	Panama City	2011	80	264	866	concrete	residential
96	SunTrust Plaza	Atlanta	1993	60	264	866	concrete	office
97	Tower Palace Three, Tower G	Seoul	2004	73	264	865	composite	residential
98	Trump World Tower	New York	2001	72	262	861	concrete	residential
99	Water Tower Place	Chicago	1976	74	262	859	concrete	residential/hotel/retail
100	Grand Gateway Plaza I	Shanghai	2005	54	262	859	concrete	office
100	Grand Gateway Plaza II	Shanghai	2005	54	262	859	concrete	office

Index of
Buildings

100 11th Avenue, *New York, USA;* 40
1075 Peachtree, *Atlanta, USA;* 72
1450 Brickell, *Miami, USA;* 47
235 Van Buren, *Chicago, USA;* 42
300 East Randolph, *Chicago, USA;* 44
353 North Clark Street, *Chicago, USA;* 72
39 Conduit Road, *Hong Kong, China;* 114
400 George Street, *Brisbane, Australia;* 100
510 Madison, *New York, USA;* 72
785 Eighth Avenue, *New York, USA;* 46

The Address, *Dubai, UAE;* 160
Al Bidda Tower, *Doha, Qatar;* 154
Al Salam Tecom Tower, *Dubai, UAE;* 160
Al Tijaria Tower, *Kuwait City, Kuwait;* 156
Aqua Tower, *Chicago, USA;* 28
Arraya Office Tower, *Kuwait City, Kuwait;*
        158

Banco Real Santander Headquarters, *São
        Paulo, Brazil;* 48
The Bank of America Tower, *New York,
        USA;* 22
BEA Financial Tower, *Shanghai, China;* 102
Boulevard Plaza, *Dubai, UAE;* 160
Broadcasting Place, *Leeds, UK;* 118
The Brooklyner, *New York, USA;* 73
BUMPS, *Beijing, China;* 104
Burj Khalifa, *Dubai, UAE;* 144

Caja Madrid Tower, *Madrid, Spain;* 132
Candle House, *Leeds, UK;* 140
Cassa, *New York, USA;* 49
China Diamond Exchange Center, *Shanghai,
        China;* 106
City Square Residences, *Singapore;* 114
The Clare at Water Tower, *Chicago, USA;* 50
Cosmopolitan Resort & Casino, *Las Vegas,
        USA;* 73
Crown Hotel at City of Dreams, *Macau,
        China;* 107

Deloitte Centre, *Auckland, New Zealand;* 108

The Elysian, *Chicago, USA;* 73

Fairmont Pacific Rim, *Vancouver, Canada;*
        51
Freeport-McMoRan Center, *Phoenix, USA;*
        52

Hegau Tower, *Singen, Germany;* 124

Imperia Tower, *Moscow, Russia;* 140
iSQUARE, *Hong Kong, China;* 84

Kalpataru Towers, *Mumbai, India;* 114
Kwun Tong 223, *Hong Kong, China;* 115

LA Live Hotel and Residences, *Los Angeles,
        USA;* 54
The Legacy, *Chicago, USA;* 56

Maastoren, *Rotterdam, The Netherlands;* 140
Mandarin Oriental, *Las Vegas, USA;* 57
Marina Bay Sands Integrated Resort,
        Singapore; 88
The Masterpiece, *Hong Kong, China;* 115
Met 2, *Miami, USA;* 74
The Mill and Jerwood Dance House, *Ipswich,
        UK;* 141
MOSAIC, *Beijing, China;* 110
Mosfilmovskaya, *Moscow, Russia;* 134

Nanjing Greenland Financial Center,
        Nanjing, China; 92
Nassima Tower, *Dubai, UAE;* 161
NHN Green Factory, *Seongnam, South
        Korea;* 111
Northeast Asia Trade Tower, *Incheon, South
        Korea;* 96

O-14, *Dubai, UAE;* 150
Ocean Heights, *Dubai, UAE;* 159
One Madison Park, *New York, USA;* 32
Opernturm, *Frankfurt, Germany;* 141

PalaisQuartier Office Tower, *Frankfurt,
        Germany;* 128
Pinnacle @ Duxton, *Singapore;* 78

RBC Centre, *Toronto, Canada;* 58
Residences at the Ritz-Carlton, *Philadelphia,
        USA;* 74

Sackville-Dundas Residences, *Toronto,
        Canada;* 59
Sama Tower, *Dubai, UAE;* 161
Santos Place, *Brisbane, Australia;* 112
Sea Towers, *Gdynia, Poland;* 141
Shangri-la, *Vancouver, Canada;* 60
Songdo First World Towers, *Incheon, South
        Korea;* 113
The St. Francis Shangri-la Place,
        Mandaluyong City, Philippines; 115
Stadthaus, *London, UK;* 136
The Standard, *New York, USA;* 62
Strata SE1, *London, UK;* 138

Terminus 200, *Atlanta, USA;* 74
theWit Hotel, *Chicago, USA;* 63

Tiffany Tower, *Dubai, UAE;* 161
Titanium La Portada, *Santiago, Chile;* 64
Toren, *New York, USA;* 66
Torre Libertad, *Mexico City, Mexico;* 67
Trump SoHo Hotel, *New York, USA;* 75
Two Alliance Center, *Atlanta, USA;* 75

Vdara Hotel & Spa, *Las Vegas, USA;* 68
Veer Towers, *Las Vegas, USA;* 36
Ventura Corporate Towers, *Rio de Janeiro,
        Brazil;* 69

W Hoboken, *Hoboken, USA;* 75
William Beaver House, *New York, USA;* 70

299 Burrard Landing; 51
785 Partners, LLC; 46

Abbott Industries, Inc; 28
Abdulsalam Alrafi Group; 160
Abraham Senerman Lamas; 64
ACCO; 54
ACICO Construction; 161
Adamson Associates; 22, 36, 57
Adam Tihany Associates; 57
ADI Limited; 106
Advanced Mechanical Systems, Inc; 28, 73
AECOM; 50
Aedas Ltd; 88, 159, 160
AEG; 54
Aflalo & Gasperini Architects; 69
AGC Partners, LP; 74
Aguilera Ingenieros S.A.; 132
AHA Consulting Engineers; 75
Ahmadiah Contracting and Trading Company;
    158
AIK Expeditions Lumiere; 36
AJD Construction Company Inc; 75
AJD Design Partnership; 136
AKF Engineers; 40
Alan G. Davenport Wind Engineering Group;
    32
Alatec; 132
Alexej Kolubkov; 134
Alf Naman Real Estate; 40
Alfonso Larraín; 64
Al Hamid Group; 161
Al-Jazera Consultants; 156
Alliance Design Group; 112
ALT Cladding; 36, 160
Andre Balazs Properties; 62, 70
Arabtec; 144, 159, 160
architectsAlliance; 59
Architectural Bureau of Sergey Skuratov; 134
Architekturbüro Andrzej Kapuscik; 141
ARC Studio Architecture + Urbanism; 78
Ardmore; 140
Arquing; 132
Arquitectonica; 48, 73, 107
Arup; 88, 96, 102, 107, 111, 114, 115
Associated International Hotels Ltd; 84
Atelier Jean Nouvel; 40
Atkins; 160, 161
Aurecon; 108
AXXA Group Ltd; 114

BAM; 128
Bank of America; 22
Barrett, Woodyard and Associates Inc; 74
Bates Smart; 107
Bayrock Group LLC; 75
Baytur; 160
BBG-BBGM; 68
Beck Group; 75
Beijing Guo Rong Real Estate Development
    Ltd; 110
Beijing New Era Architectural Design Ltd; 104

Beijing Xinfengxinde Real-Estate Development
    Co Ltd; 104
Beijing Zihexin Plaza Co Ltd; 104
Belhasa Engineering & Contracting Co; 160
Benoy Ltd; 84
Besix Group; 140, 144, 160
Beyer Blinder Belle Architects; 40
BFC; 66
BFLS; 138
BGS; 141
B+H Architects; 58
Bollinger Grohmann; 141
Boundary Layer Wind Tunnel Laboratory; 144
Bovis Lend Lease; 32, 42, 50, 70, 72, 73, 75
Brasfield & Gorrie; 72
Brockett/Davis/Drake Inc; 74
Brookfield Developments; 138
Brookfield Multiplex; 108
BRT Architekten; 161
BTS; 69
Buro Happold; 140
Butler Partners; 112
BWL Projekt Sp.zo.o.; 141

Cadillac Fairview Corporation Limited; 58
Camargo Corrêa Desenvolvimento Imobiliário;
    69
Cape Advisors, Inc; 40
CareyJones Architects; 140
Casas+Architects; 115
Case Foundation; 28
Castle House Developments Ltd; 138
CDC; 47
Central Park East Associates, LLC; 52
Cerami & Associates; 66
Cetra/CRI Architecture PLLC; 32
CetraRuddy; 32, 49
Chip Eng Seng Contractors (1988) Pte Ltd; 78
Cini-Little International; 44
City Developments Ltd; 114
CL3; 88
Clarett Group; 73
CMK Companies, Ltd; 42
Coastal Construction; 47
Commercial Real Estate Company; 156
Constructora SENARCO; 64
Cook+Fox Architects LLP; 22
Cosentini Associates; 42, 44, 68, 73, 75, 113
Cosmopolitan of Las Vegas; 73
Cousins Properties Inc; 74
Cox Rayner Architects; 100
CPP Wind Engineering Consultants; 46
Creekside Development Corporation; 150
C.S. Associates; 44, 56
Curtain Wall Design & Consulting, Inc; 68
CYVSA; 67

Daewoo; 96
Dam & Partners Architecten; 140
Damac Gulf Properties LLC; 159
Daniel Corporation; 72
Daniels Corporation; 59
Daniel Weinbach and Associates; 73

Dave Pearson Architects Limited; 108
Davis Langdon & Seah Ltd; 84, 115, 140
Dennis Lau & Ng Chun Man Architects and
    Engineers (HK) Ltd; 114, 115
Design/Build; 63
DeSimone Consulting Engineers; 40, 47, 49, 62,
    68, 70, 73, 75
Dimensions Engineering Consultants; 161
Dongyang Structural; 96
Donovan Hill; 112
DONSTROY Corporation; 134
Downing; 118
DS Development; 134
Dubai Contracting Company LLC; 150, 161
Dubai World; 36
Duda/Paine Architects LLP; 74
Durst Organization; 22

Easewin Development Ltd & Morison Ltd; 115
Ebener & Partner; 141
ECADI; 92, 102
ECD Company; 63
ECG Engineering Consultants Group; 159
Edwards & Zuck Engineers; 62
EEI Corporation; 115
EFCO Corp.; 28
Elysian Development Group – Chicago LLC; 73
Emaar Properties PJSC; 144, 160
Emcor Limited; 141
Emmer Pfenninger Partner AG; 132
Enermodal Engineering Ltd; 58
Enka Insaat ve Sanayi A.S.; 140
Ennead Architects; 62
Enrique Martinex Romero; 67
Environmental Systems Design, Inc; 72
Envirospace Consultants Pte Ltd; 78
Epstein; 72
ERGA Progress; 150
Esplanade Capital; 46
Ettinger Engineering Consultants; 46
Evans Kuhn & Associates Inc; 52

FCC – ACS; 132
FEA Consulting Engineers; 73
Feilden Clegg Bradley Studios; 118
Feitosa e Cruz; 48
Fentress Architects; 158
First Elysian Properties LLC; 73
FKN. GaTech; 124
Foster + Partners; 132
Franciscan Sisters of Chicago Service
    Corporation; 50
Friedmutter Group; 73
Front; 49

Gale International; 96, 113
Gamble McKinnon Green; 112
Gammon Construction Ltd; 84
Gaopeng (Shanghai) Real Estate Development
    Co Ltd; 102
GDO GROUP; 140
Gensler; 54
George Downing Construction; 118

George Floth Pty Ltd; 100
GHD Global Pty Ltd; 154
Gilsanz Murray Steficek LLP; 72, 132
GKV Architects; 73
Goettsch Partners; 44, 106
Goldstein Associates PLLC; 75
Gonzalo Martinez-Pita Copello; 132
Goregaokar Architects; 114
Gotham Construction; 40
Graziani + Corazza Architects Inc; 59
Great Lakes; 73
Greystone Communities; 50
Grosvenor Australia Investments Pty Ltd; 100
Ground Engineering Consultants, Inc; 28
Grupo Ideurban; 67
Gurtz Electric Company; 28, 73
GVV Singen; 124
Gwathmey Siegel & Associates Architects LLC; 75

H.A. Bader; 62
Halcrow Yolles; 36, 57, 58, 118
Halvorson and Partners; 63, 73, 132
Han Bang UBIS Co; 111
Handel Architects LLP; 74, 75
Hardin Construction; 74
Harley Hadow; 141
Hastie International; 161
Health Care Service Corporation; 44
Heerim Architects; 96
Henderson Land Development Co Ltd; 114, 115
Heng Lai Construction Co Ltd; 115
Heng Shung Construction Co Ltd; 114
Herrick Steel; 54
HE Simms; 118
HGOR Landscape Architects and Planners; 74
hhpberlin – Ingenieure für Brandschutz; 128
Higgs & Hill; 154
Hill International; 154
Hip Hing Builders Co Ltd; 115
Hirsch Bender Associates; 88
HKS Inc; 74
HNGS Engineers; 74
Hoerr Schaudt Landscape Architecture; 50
Holder Construction; 52
Holmes Consulting Group; 108
Housing & Development Board, Singapore; 78
Hutchinson Builders; 112
Hyder Consulting; 144, 160
Hyundai Engineering & Construction; 111

Ian Banham & Associates Consulting
    Engineers; 159
IB Schwarz; 124
IE Consultants, Inc; 28
IFFCO; 161
I.M. Robbins Consulting Engineers; 70, 72
Infinity World Development Corporation; 57
Ingenieursbureau Zonneveld BV; 140
Inmobiliaria Titanium S.A.; 64
Integrated Energy Concepts; 66
Invest Komfort SA; 141
Ironstate Development Company; 75

I. Shipetin Design Bureau; 134
ISIS Waterside Regeneration; 140
Ismael Leyva Architects, PC; 46
Israel Berger & Associates; 32, 36, 66, 74, 75

James K.M. Cheng Architects Inc; 51, 60
Jaros, Baum & Bolles Consulting Engineers; 22
Javier Martin Minguez; 132
Jenkins & Huntington; 44, 49
Jiangsu Suzhong Construction Group Co Ltd;
    104
JKMF; 69
John Buck Company; 62
John Lyall Architects; 141
Jones Kwong Kishi Consulting; 51, 60
Jordan & Skala Engineers; 72
Jose Aliling & Associates; 115
J Roger Preston Limited; 107

Kalpataru Group; 114
KBK #11 Ventures Ltd; 60
Kevan Shaw; 156
KFM Partnership; 112
KGA Trinity Chambers; 118
Khatib and Associates; 28
Kimley-Horn; 47, 74
KLH, UK; 136
Klimaster Sp.zo.o.; 141
Kohn Pedersen Fox Associates; 57, 58, 69, 96,
    113, 164
Koo and Associates Ltd; 63
KSP Juergen Engel Architekten GmbH; 128
Kunwon Architect; 113
KWP Ltd (Beijing); 102
Kyungjai Structural Engineers; 111

Laing O'Rourke; 141
Langan Engineering & Environmental Services;
    46, 62
Laskin & Associates; 52
Las Vegas Sands Corporation; 88
Ledcor Construction Ltd; 60
Leeds Metropolitan University; 118
Leigh & Orange; 107
Leighton-China State-John Holland, JV; 107
Leighton Properties Pty Ltd; 100
Leo A. Daly; 68
Lerch Bates & Associates; 36, 92, 144
L.F. Driscoll Co; 74
LGA Engineering Inc; 75
Light Works; 108
Lincolne Scott; 112
LKM Consulting Engineers; 59
Lochsa Engineering LLC; 68
Lockwood, Andrews & Newnam, Inc; 68
Loewenberg Architects, LLC; 28
Lohan Anderson LLC; 72
Lovejoy; 140
L-Plan Lichtplanung; 36
Lucien Lagrange Architects LTD; 73

MAB Development Deutschland GmbH; 128
M.ACICO Real Estate Agent LLC; 161

Macklowe Properties; 72
Mack Scogin Merrill Elam Architects; 75
Magellan Development Group; 28
Magnusson Klemencic Associates; 28, 44
Martin & Martin; 73
Masterclima; 64
Matthew & Goodman; 118
McDaniel Fire System; 28
McGuire Igleski; 56
McHugh Construction; 28, 50, 63, 73
Meinhardt Ltd; 84, 114, 115, 159
Melco Crown Entertainment Limited; 107
Melillo & Bauer; 75
Mercury Engineering Polska Sp.zo.o.; 141
Mesirow Financial; 52, 72
Metropolitan Housing Trust; 136
MG Engineering; 32, 49
MGM Mirage Design Group; 36, 57, 68
MHA Engenharia Ltda; 48, 69
Michael Popper and Associates; 136
Miranda&Nasi; 64
Mitchell Partnership; 58
Modzelewski + Rodek Sp.zo.o.; 141
MOED de ARMAS & SHANNON Architects;
    72
Monroe/Wabash Development LLC; 56
Morgan Ashurst; 141
Mott Connell Ltd; 107
MOW Generalplanung; 141
M. Paul Friedberg and Partners; 70
MPC Planning; 108
M/S Al Rostamani Pegel; 161
Mulvey & Banani Intl.; 58
Murphy/Jahn Architects; 36, 124
Murray Company; 54

Nabih Youssef Associates; 54
Nanjing State Owned Assets & Greenland
    Financial Center Co Ltd; 92
Nation Sheen Ltd & Carry Express Investment
    Ltd; 114
NBBJ; 111, 140
Nemetz (S/A) & Associates Ltd; 51, 60
Neo Pharma Pvt Ltd; 114
New World Development Co Ltd; 115
NHN Corporation; 111
Nichols, Brosch, Wurst, Wolfe & Associates
    Inc; 47, 74
Nielson Properties; 112
Norman Disney & Young; 108, 112
NORR Group; 156
Norwin AS; 138

OAP; 115
One Lux Studio; 44
Ong & Ong Pte Ltd; 114
Opernplatz Property Holdings GmbH & Co
    KG; 141
OVG projectontwikkeling BV; 140

Pan Arab Consulting Engineers; 158
Park Place Holdings at Brickell LLC; 47
Parsons Brinckerhoff Pte Ltd; 88, 114, 115

Paul Koehler Consulting Structural Engineers; 52
Pavarini McGovern; 49, 62
PBS&J; 47
PCL Constructors; 58
Pelli Clarke Pelli Architects; 67
Pennoni Associates Inc; 74
Perini Building Company; 36, 57, 68, 73
Perkins+Will; 42, 50
Peter Berchtold Engineering Consultants; 128
Peterson Holdings Co Ltd; 114
Peterson Investment Group Inc; 51
Peter Walker & Partners Landscape Architects; 88
P & G Tract "C" Development Ltd; 74
Phillips Farevaag Smallenberg; 51, 60
Platinum Tower Co; 154
POSCO Engineering & Construction Co Ltd; 113
Powell-Harpstead Inc; 74
Prairie Material Services, Inc; 28
Pravin Gala & Associates; 114
Price and Myers; 141
Profit System Development Ltd; 115
Prof. Mäckler Architekten; 141
Protek; 111

Qatari Arabian Construction Company; 154
Qingdao Construction Group Co; 110

R.A. Heintges & Associates; 150
Ramboll; 140
Record Sp.zo.o.; 141
Reiser + Umemoto, RUR Architecture, PC; 150
Repsol YPF; 132
Resource Coordination Partnership; 112
R.G. Vanderweil, LLP; 88
RHR Consulting Engineers; 73
Rider Levett Bucknall; 108, 112, 115
Ridge and Partners; 118
Rilea Group; 47
RJA Group, Inc; 73, 92, 144
RKM Design Consultants; 44
Robert Bird Group; 100
Robert Myers Associates; 118
Rocco Design Architects Ltd; 84
Ron Rumble; 112
RS-AK; 141
RSP Architects Planners & Engineers Pte Ltd; 78
RTKL Associates; 47, 74
Rule Joy Trammell + Rubio LLC; 72
RV Architecture, LLC; 68
RWDI, Inc; 92, 138, 144

Saegil E&C; 111
Safdie Architects; 88
SAKO Architects; 104, 110
Salhia Real Estate Company; 158
Samoo Architects & Engineers; 111
Samsung; 144, 160
Sapir Organization; 75
SASCO; 54

Schaaf Glass Co; 28
Schaeffers Consulting Engineers; 58
Schirmer Engineering; 160
Schreiber Ingenieure; 124
SDL Structural Engineers; 75
SDS Investments LLC; 70
SEB Investment GmbH; 140
Selig Enterprises; 72
Severud Associates Consulting Engineers; 22, 66
Shanghai Construction Group; 92
Shanghai Lujiazui Development Co Ltd; 106
Shanghai New Century Co Ltd; 106
Shanghai No. 2 Construction Co Ltd; 106
Shanghai No. 7 Construction Co Ltd; 102
Shanghai Tong-qing Technologic Development Co Ltd; 106
Shanghai Zhong-fu Architects; 106
Shang Properties, Inc; 115
Shawn Hausman, Roman & Williams; 62
SHBC Contracting Company; 156
Sigmund Soudack & Associates Inc; 59
SIRVE; 64
Skidmore, Owings & Merrill LLP; 66, 92, 144
Slazer Enterprises; 32
SLCE Architects, LLP; 70, 72
Smallwood, Reynolds, Stewart, Stewart & Associates Inc; 75
SmithGroup; 52
SMW; 49
Solly Assa; 49
Solomon Cordwell Buenz; 56
Soltos; 111
SPD LLC; 72
Ssangyong; 88
Stanley D. Lindsey & Associates Ltd; 72
Stephen Cheng Consulting Engineers Ltd; 114, 115
Sterling, Cooper & Associates; 51, 60
Steven Feller PE; 47
Strybos Barron King Ltd; 58
STS Consultants; 50, 92, 144
Studio Gang Architects, Ltd; 28
Suffolk Construction Company Inc; 74
Sun Hung Kai Properties Ltd; 115
Sunjin Mechanical Consultant; 111
Sunrex; 111
Surbana International Consultants Pte Ltd; 78
SWA Group; 92, 144
Sweeny Sterling Finlayson & Co Architects Inc; 58

Team 73 HK Ltd; 115
Techdesign; 141
Techniker Ltd; 136
Techniplan Adviseurs BV; 140
Techno Group; 114
Telford Homes; 136
TEMON Técnica de Montagens e Construções Ltda; 48
TEN Arquitectos; 49
Terra Engineering, Ltd; 42
TFP Farrells Limited; 102

THERMOPLAN Engenharia Térmica Ltda; 48
Thiess Pty Ltd; 100
Thornton Tomasetti; 50, 74, 113
Times Square Construction, Inc; 46
Tishman Construction; 22, 36, 72
Tishman Speyer; 69, 75, 141
Tonkin & Taylor; 108
Toronto Community Housing Corporation; 59
Towers/Golde; 113
Transsolar; 124
Trump Organization; 75
TsAO & McKOWN Architects; 70
Turner International; 144
T.Y. Lin International Pte Ltd; 78
Tylk Gustafson Reckers Wilson Andrews, LLC; 42

Urban Renewal Authority; 115
URS Corporation Ltd; 138

Van Deusen & Associates; 32, 66
Vis a Vis Design Studio; 141
VSN Engineers; 74

Walsh Associates; 141
Walsh Construction; 44, 56
Warren and Mahoney; 108
Washington Fiuza; 48
Waterscape LLC; 49
Waugh Thistleton Architects; 136
Webcor; 54
Weischede, Herrmann und Partner; 128
Werner Sobek Ingenieure; 36, 124
Westbank Project Corp.; 51
Western States; 54
Wharfside Properties; 141
WMA Consulting Engineers; 50, 56
Woh Hup Pte Ltd; 114
Wolff Landscape Architecture, Inc; 28
Wong and Tung International Ltd; 115
Woods Bagot; 108
WSP Cantor Seinuk; 32, 73
WSP Flack + Kurtz; 36, 57, 74
WSP Group; 115, 138
WTorre Empreendimentos Imobiliários S.A.; 48
WTorre Engenharia; 48

Ysrael A. Seinuk, PC; 46, 74, 150, 170

ZAO "Fleiner-City"; 140
Züblin; 124, 141

Image
Credits

CTBUH Organizational
Structure & Members

Pickard Chilton Architects, Inc
RISE International, LLC
RMJM – Hillier
Rolf Jensen & Associates, Inc
Rosenwasser/Grossman Consulting Engineers, PC
Rowan Williams Davies & Irwin, Inc
Schirmer Engineering Corp
SIAPLAN Architects and Planners
Solomon Cordwell Buenz
Studio Gang Architects
SWA Group
Thornton Tomasetti, Inc
Viracon, Inc
Walter P. Moore and Associates, Inc
Werner Voss + Partner
Willis Group
Woods Bagot

Contributors
Aedas, Ltd
ALHOSN University
Alvine Engineering
American Iron and Steel Institute
Barker Mohandas, LLC
Bonacci Group
Bovis Lend Lease
Broadway Malyan
Canary Wharf Group, PLC
Canderel Management, Inc
CB Engineers
Continental Automated Buildings Association
CS Structural Engineering, Inc
DeStefano + Partners, Ltd
DHV Bouw en Industrie
Dong Yang Structural Engineers
Dow Corning Corp.
The Durst Organization, Inc
Gardner Metal Systems, Inc
Goettsch Partners
Hughes Associates, Inc
INTEMAC, SA
Jacobs
JCE Structural Engineering Group, Inc
KHP Konig und Heunisch Planungsgesellschaft
MulvannyG2 Architecture
Nabih Youssef & Associates
National Fire Protection Assocation
Norman Disney & Young
Perkins + Will
Permasteelisa North America
SAMOO Architects & Engineers
Schindler Elevator Corp.
SilverEdge Systems Software, Inc
The Steel Institute of New York
Structal-Heavy Steel Construction
T. R. Hamzah & Yeang Sdn. Bhd.
Tekla Corp.
ThyssenKrupp Elevator, Qatar
TSNIIEP for Residential and Public Buildings
WH-P GmbH Beratende Ingenieure
Wilkinson Eyre Architects

Participants
Aidea Philippines, Inc
AKF Group, LLC

Al Ghurair Construction – Aluminium LLC
Al Jazera Consultants
Allford Hall Monaghan Morris, Ltd
Altus Group, Ltd
Architectural Design and Research Institute of Tongji University (Group) Co, Ltd
ARC Studio Architecture + Urbanism
ArcelorMittal
Architects 61 Pte, Ltd
Architectural Institute of Korea
Arquitectonica International Corp.
W.S. Atkins & Partners Overseas
BAUM Architects, Engineers & Consultants, Inc
BG&E Pty, Ltd
Billings Design Associates, Ltd
Boston Properties, Inc
Bouygues Construction
Breuer Consulting Group
Building Design International, Inc
Callison, LLP
CBM Engineers, Inc
CDC Curtain Wall Design & Consulting, Inc
Chicago Committee on High-rise Buildings
China Academy of Building Research
CityLife, SRL
Code Consultants, Inc
Contract Glaziers, Inc
Conwood Realty Pvt, Ltd
COWI A/S
CPP, Inc
CS Associates, Inc
CTL Group
Cundall
Dagher Engineering, PLLC
Dar Al-Handasah (Shair & Partners)
Delft University of Technology
Dennis Lau & Ng Chun Man Architects & Engineers (HK), Ltd
dhk Architects Pty, Ltd
DSP Design Associates Pvt, Ltd
Dunbar & Boardman
Edgett Williams Consulting Group, Inc
Environmental Systems Design, Inc
Epstein
Faithful + Gould
Fortune Consultants, Ltd
FXFOWLE Architects, LLC
GHC Brydens Project Management
Glass Wall Systems
Godrej Properties, Ltd.
Gold Coast City Council
Gorproject (Urban Planning Institute of Residential and Public Buildings)
Guangzhou Scientific Computing Consultants Co, Ltd
GVK Elevator Consulting Services, Inc
Halvorson and Partners
Hamza Associates
Haynes-Whaley Associates, Inc
Heller Manus Architects
Hilson Moran Partnership, Ltd
Hoerr Schaudt Landscape Architects
HOK, Inc
Hong Kong Housing Authority
Horvath Reich CDC, Inc
Hycrete, Inc
Intelligent Engineering
Irwinconsult Pty, Ltd

Iv-Consult b.v.
JBA Consulting Engineers, Inc
John Portman & Associates, Inc
KEO International Consultants, Inc
The Korean Structural Engineers Association
KPMB Architects
Langan Engineering & Environmental Services, Inc
Leigh & Orange, Ltd
Lerch Bates, Inc
Lobby Agency
Lucien Lagrange Architects
Magellan Development Group, LLC
Magnetek, Inc
Margolin Bros. Engineering & Consulting, Ltd
McNamara / Salvia, Inc
MechoShade Systems, Inc
Middlebrook + Louie Structural Engineers
Murphy/Jahn
Nikken Sekkei, Ltd
Nishkian Menninger Consulting and Structural Engineers
O'Connor Sutton Cronnin
Odell Associates, Inc
Option One International, WLL
Otis Elevator Company
P&T Group
Palafox Associates
PDW Architects
Pelli Clarke Pelli Architects
Perkins Eastman Architects, PC
Powe Architects
PPG Industries, Inc
Rafael Vinoly Architects, PC
Redix, Ltd
Rene Lagos y Asociados
Riggio / Boron, Ltd
Rodium Properties
Ronald Lu & Partners
Sematic Italia, SpA
Stanley D. Lindsey & Associates, Ltd
Stauch Vorster Architects
Stephan Reinke Architects, Ltd
Steven Holl Architects
Studio Altieri S.P.A.
Syska Hennessy Group, Inc
Takenaka Corporation
Taylor Thomson Whitting Pty, Ltd
TFP Farrells, Ltd
The Trump Organization
Thermafiber, Inc
Trainor Glass Company
Transsolar
United States Gypsum Corp.
University of Nottingham
Vanguard Realty Pvt, Ltd
Vipac Engineers & Scientists, Ltd
VOA Associates, Inc
Walsh Construction Company
Werner Sobek Stuttgart GmbH & Co, KG
Windtech Consultants Pty, Ltd
WOHA Architects Pte, Ltd
Wong & Ouyang (HK), Ltd
Wordsearch
World Academy of Sciences for Complex Safety
WSP Cantor Seinuk
WSP Flack + Kurtz, Inc
WTM Engineers International GmbH
Y. A. Yashar Architects

Supporting Contributors are those who contribute $10,000; Patrons: $6,000; Donors: $3,000; Contributors: $1,500; Participants: $750.